INSIDE THE MIND Exploring Anxiety Disorders

Written by Andrew D Beattie

2023

INSIDE THE MIND - Exploring Anxiety Disorders

Mental Health

Andrew D Beattie

Published by Andrew D Beattie, 2023.

Table Of Contents

13**Ta**

bleOfContents

INSIDE THE MIND - EXPLORING ANXIETY DISORDERS

55

69

Inside the Mind: Exploring A - Z of Anxiety Disorders

Inside the Mind: Exploring Anxiety Disorders

Inside the Mind: Exploring Anxiety Disorders

Inside the Mind: Exploring A - Z of Anxiety Disorders

Chapter 1: Understanding Anxiety Disorders

Defining Anxiety Disorders

Chapter 1: Understanding Anxiety Disorders

Defining Anxiety Disorders

Anxiety is a common emotion that everyone experiences from time to time. It is a natural response to stress or a perceived threat, helping us to stay alert and focused. However, for some individuals, anxiety can become overwhelming and debilitating, interfering with daily life and overall well-being.

These individuals may be suffering from anxiety disorders.

Anxiety disorders encompass a wide range of conditions characterized by excessive and persistent worry, fear, and nervousness. They are more than just feeling anxious in certain situations; they involve a constant state of unease that can be dif cult to control or alleviate. In this subchapter, we will explore the A-Z of anxiety disorders, shedding light on the various conditions that fall under this umbrella term.

From agoraphobia to social anxiety disorder, panic disorder to generalized anxiety disorder, each anxiety disorder has its unique symptoms, triggers, and impacts on an individual's life. For example, someone with agoraphobia may have an intense fear of being in situations where escape might be dif cult or help might not be available, leading them to avoid crowded places, public transportation, or even leaving their homes. On the other hand, individuals suffering from social anxiety disorder experience extreme self-consciousness in social situations and fear being judged or humiliated by others.

It is crucial to understand that anxiety disorders are not simply a result of personal weakness or character aws. They are real, treatable medical conditions, often in uenced by a combination of genetic, environmental, and psychological factors. Anxiety disorders can affect individuals of all ages, genders, and backgrounds, and they should never be dismissed or stigmatized.

In this chapter, we will not only delve into the speci c symptoms and diagnostic criteria for each anxiety disorder but also explore the available treatments and coping strategies. It is important for the general public to have a comprehensive understanding of anxiety disorders, as they are more prevalent than one might think. By increasing awareness and knowledge, we can foster empathy and support for those who are affected by these conditions, helping them seek appropriate help and lead ful lling lives.

Throughout this book, we aim to provide a comprehensive guide to the A-Z of anxiety disorders, shedding light on their causes, symptoms, and available treatments. By exploring the intricate workings of the mind and the complexities of anxiety disorders, we hope to empower individuals to recognize and address their own anxiety struggles or support their loved ones in nding the help they need. Together, we can break the stigma surrounding anxiety disorders and promote mental well-being for all.

Common Symptoms of Anxiety Disorders

Common Symptoms of Anxiety

Disorders

Anxiety disorders are a group of mental health conditions that affect millions of people worldwide. These disorders can manifest in various ways, leading to distress and impairment in daily life. Understanding the common symptoms of anxiety disorders is crucial to recognizing and seeking appropriate treatment for these conditions.

1. Excessive Worry: One of the hallmark symptoms of anxietydisorders is persistent and excessive worry or fear. Individuals with anxiety disorders often nd it challenging to control their worrying thoughts, which can lead to restlessness and irritability.
2. Restlessness and Nervousness: People with anxietydisorders may experience a constant feeling of restlessness or nervousness. They may feel on edge, be easily startled, or have dif culty relaxing.
3. Physical Symptoms: Anxiety disorders can also manifest inphysical symptoms such as rapid heartbeat, sweating, trembling, shortness of breath,

dizziness, and chest pain. These symptoms can be mistaken for a heart attack or other physical illnesses, leading to unnecessary medical tests and anxiety.

4. Sleep Problems: Anxiety disorders frequently disrupt sleeppatterns, causing dif culties falling asleep, staying asleep, or experiencing restful sleep. Insomnia is a common symptom, often exacerbating other anxiety-related symptoms.

5. Avoidance Behavior: Individuals with anxiety disorders maybegin to avoid certain situations or places that trigger their anxiety. This avoidance behavior can signi cantly impact their daily lives, leading to isolation and dif culties in social, academic, or occupational domains.

6. Panic Attacks: Panic attacks are sudden episodes of intensefear or discomfort, accompanied by physical symptoms such as a racing heart, sweating, trembling, shortness of breath, and a feeling of impending doom. Panic attacks can be extremely distressing and may occur unexpectedly or in response to speci c triggers.

7. Obsessive-Compulsive Symptoms: Some anxiety disorders,such as obsessive-compulsive disorder (OCD), involve recurring, intrusive thoughts (obsessions) and repetitive behaviors or rituals (compulsions). These symptoms can consume signi cant amounts of time and interfere with daily functioning.

8. Phobias: Anxiety disorders can also manifest as speci cphobias, where individuals experience an intense

fear of a particular object, situation, or activity. Common phobias include heights, spiders, ying, or enclosed spaces.

9. Social Anxiety: Social anxiety disorder causes intense fearand anxiety in social situations, leading to avoidance of social interactions or signi cant distress when forced to participate. This can impact relationships, career opportunities, and overall quality of life.

10. Generalized Anxiety: Generalized anxiety disorder (GAD) involves excessive worry and anxiety about various aspects of life, such as work, health, nances, or relationships. Individuals with GAD nd it challenging to control their worries, often anticipating the worst outcomes.

Recognizing these common symptoms of anxiety disorders is the rst step towards seeking help and support. If you or someone you know experiences these symptoms, it is essential to consult a mental health professional for an accurate diagnosis and appropriate treatment. Remember, anxiety disorders are highly treatable, and with the right interventions, individuals can regain control of their lives and experience improved well-being.

Prevalence and Impact of Anxiety Disorders

Prevalence and Impact of Anxiety Disorders

INSIDE THE MIND - EXPLORING ANXIETY DISORDERS

Anxiety disorders are a common mental health condition that affects millions of people worldwide. In this subchapter, we will explore the prevalence and impact of anxiety disorders, shedding light on the various types of these disorders and their effects on individuals and society as a whole.

Anxiety disorders encompass a wide range of conditions, including generalized anxiety disorder (GAD), panic disorder, social anxiety disorder (SAD), phobias, and post-traumatic stress disorder (PTSD), among others. These disorders are characterized by excessive and persistent worry, fear, and apprehension, often leading to signi cant distress and impairment in daily functioning.

The prevalence of anxiety disorders is staggering. According to the World Health Organization, around 1 in 13 people globally suffer from anxiety, making it one of the most prevalent mental health disorders. It affects people of all ages, genders, and backgrounds, with symptoms typically manifesting in adolescence or early adulthood.

The impact of anxiety disorders can be far-reaching, affecting various aspects of a person's life. Individuals with anxiety disorders often experience physical symptoms such as rapid heartbeat, shortness of breath, sweating, and muscle tension. These symptoms can lead to avoidance behaviors, isolating individuals from social activities, work, or school.

Moreover, anxiety disorders can have a signi cant impact on mental well-being, leading to feelings of depression, low selfesteem, and a reduced quality of life. The constant worry and fear associated with these disorders can also strain relationships with family, friends, and colleagues.

On a societal level, anxiety disorders result in a substantial economic burden. The costs of healthcare services, lost productivity, and decreased work performance due to anxiety-related issues are substantial. Furthermore, anxiety disorders often coexist with other mental health conditions, such as depression or substance abuse, further complicating treatment and increasing the burden on healthcare systems.

Understanding the prevalence and impact of anxiety disorders is crucial for the general public. By increasing awareness and knowledge about these conditions, we can reduce stigma and promote early diagnosis and effective treatment options. Additionally, providing support and empathy to individuals affected by anxiety disorders can play a vital role in helping them navigate their challenges and improve their overall wellbeing.

In the subsequent chapters of this book, we will delve into the A-Z of anxiety disorders, exploring each condition in detail, including its symptoms, causes, and available treatment options. By gaining a comprehensive understanding of anxiety disorders, we can empower ourselves and others to foster a more compassionate and inclusive society.

Misconceptions about Anxiety Disorders

Misconceptions about Anxiety

Disorders

Anxiety disorders are among the most common mental health conditions, affecting millions of people worldwide. However, despite their prevalence, there are numerous misconceptions surrounding these disorders that often contribute to misunderstandings and stigmatization. In this subchapter, we will debunk some of the most common misconceptions about anxiety disorders to help the general public gain a better understanding of these conditions.

Inside the Mind: Exploring A - Z of Anxiety Disorders

Inside the Mind: Exploring Anxiety Disorders

One common misconception is that anxiety disorders are simply a result of being weak or lacking willpower. In reality, anxiety disorders are complex conditions that involve a combination of genetic, environmental, and biological factors. They are not a re ection of an individual's character or strength. Understanding this can help reduce the stigma associated with anxiety disorders and promote empathy and support for those who are affected.

Another misconception is that anxiety disorders are just extreme forms of stress and can be easily overcome by simply "calming down." While stress can contribute to anxiety, anxiety disorders are characterized by persistent and excessive worry that can interfere with daily functioning. It is crucial to recognize that anxiety disorders are not something that individuals can simply "snap out of" or control through willpower alone. They often require professional help and treatment.

There is also a misconception that anxiety disorders only affect adults. While it is true that many anxiety disorders develop during adolescence or adulthood, they can also emerge in children and teenagers. Childhood anxiety disorders are often overlooked or dismissed as typical childhood fears or temporary phases, leading to delayed diagnosis and treatment. Raising awareness about the prevalence of anxiety disorders in children is essential to ensure early intervention and support.

Furthermore, anxiety disorders are not always visible or apparent to others. Many individuals with anxiety disorders experience internal struggles that are not easily observable. This can lead to misunderstandings and judgments, with others questioning the validity of their condition. It is important to remember that just because someone appears calm on the outside does not mean they are not experiencing intense anxiety on the inside.

Inside the Mind: Exploring Anxiety Disorders

In conclusion, debunking misconceptions about anxiety disorders is crucial for promoting understanding, empathy, and support for those affected. By dispelling the belief that anxiety disorders are a sign of weakness, highlighting the complexity of these conditions, and emphasizing that they can affect anyone regardless of age, we can contribute to a more inclusive and supportive society. It is essential to educate ourselves and others about anxiety disorders to help break down the barriers that prevent individuals from seeking help and receiving the support they need.

Chapter 2 Generalized Anxiety Disorder (GAD)

Overview of Generalized Anxiety Disorder

Chapter 2: Generalized Anxiety Disorder (GAD)

Overview of Generalized Anxiety Disorder

Generalized Anxiety Disorder (GAD) is a common mental health condition that affects millions of individuals worldwide. In this subchapter, we will explore the various aspects of GAD, shedding light on its symptoms, causes, and available treatments. Whether you are seeking information for yourself or interested in understanding the experiences of others, this overview will provide you with a comprehensive understanding of this anxiety disorder.

GAD is characterized by excessive and uncontrollable worry and anxiety about daily life events, causing signi cant distress and impairment in various areas of life. Individuals with GAD often nd it challenging to control their anxious thoughts, leading to a constant state of worry that can persist for months or even years. This chronic anxiety can impact their ability to concentrate, sleep, and carry out daily activities, affecting their overall quality of life.

Inside the Mind: Exploring Anxiety Disorders

The symptoms of GAD may vary from person to person, but common signs include restlessness, irritability, muscle tension, dif culty concentrating, and sleep disturbances. Physical symptoms such as headaches, stomachaches, and fatigue may also accompany the psychological manifestations of GAD. It is essential to remember that while occasional worry is a normal part of life, GAD involves excessive and persistent worry that is disproportionate to the situation at hand.

The causes of GAD are multifactorial and can include a combination of genetic, environmental, and neurochemical factors. Family history of anxiety disorders, traumatic life events, and imbalances in brain chemistry are some of the factors that contribute to the development of GAD. However, it is important to note that the exact cause of GAD remains unknown, and further research is needed to gain a deeper understanding of this complex disorder.

Fortunately, there are effective treatments available for individuals with GAD. Psychotherapy, such as cognitivebehavioral therapy (CBT), is commonly used to help individuals identify and challenge their anxious thoughts, develop coping mechanisms, and manage stress. Medications, such as selective serotonin reuptake inhibitors (SSRIs), may also be prescribed to alleviate symptoms of GAD.

In conclusion, GAD is a prevalent anxiety disorder characterized by excessive and uncontrollable worry. It can signi cantly impact an individual's daily life and overall wellbeing. Recognizing the symptoms, understanding the potential causes, and seeking appropriate treatment are crucial steps towards managing GAD effectively. By raising awareness and promoting understanding of this disorder, we can support individuals affected by GAD and create a more compassionate and informed society.

Causes and Risk Factors of GADCauses and Risk Factors of GAD

Inside the Mind: Exploring A - Z of Anxiety Disorders

Generalized Anxiety Disorder (GAD) is a common mental health condition that affects millions of people worldwide. While the exact cause of GAD is not fully understood, it is believed to be a result of a combination of factors, including genetics, brain chemistry, and environmental factors. Understanding the causes and risk factors of GAD can help individuals and their loved ones better recognize and manage the condition.

Genetics play a signi cant role in the development of GAD. Research suggests that individuals with a family history of anxiety disorders are more likely to develop GAD themselves. Certain genes associated with anxiety and stress responses may contribute to an increased vulnerability to developing GAD. However, it is essential to note that genetics alone are not the sole factor in the development of GAD, as other environmental and psychological factors also play a role.

Brain chemistry imbalances are another potential cause of GAD. Neurotransmitters, such as serotonin, dopamine, and gamma-aminobutyric acid (GABA), are chemicals in the brain that regulate mood and anxiety. An imbalance in these neurotransmitters can lead to increased anxiety levels and contribute to the development of GAD. Additionally, abnormalities in certain areas of the brain, such as the amygdala and prefrontal cortex, which are responsible for processing emotions and regulating fear responses, can also contribute to the development of GAD.

Environmental factors can also contribute to the development of GAD. Traumatic experiences, such as physical or emotional abuse, neglect, or the loss of a loved one, can increase the risk of developing GAD. Chronic stress, such as work-related stress, nancial dif culties, or relationship problems, can also contribute to the development of GAD. Certain personality traits, such as being highly self-critical, perfectionistic, or having a tendency to overthink, can also increase the risk of developing GAD.

It is important to recognize that anyone can develop GAD, regardless of age, gender, or background. However, by understanding the potential causes and risk factors, individuals can take steps to manage and reduce their risk of developing GAD. Seeking professional help, practicing stress management techniques, maintaining a healthy lifestyle, and building a support network of friends and family are all strategies that can help individuals cope with anxiety and reduce the risk of developing GAD.

Inside the Mind: Exploring A - Z of Anxiety Disorders

In conclusion, GAD is a complex mental health condition in uenced by a combination of genetic, brain chemistry, and environmental factors. By understanding the causes and risk factors of GAD, individuals can become more informed about the condition and take proactive steps to manage their anxiety. Remember, seeking professional help and support is essential in effectively managing GAD and improving overall well-being.

Diagnostic Criteria for GAD

Generalized Anxiety Disorder (GAD) is a common anxiety disorder that affects millions of individuals worldwide. It is characterized by excessive and uncontrollable worrying about various aspects of life, including work, health, family, and relationships. In this subchapter, we will explore the diagnostic criteria used to identify GAD and shed light on the symptoms that may indicate the presence of this disorder.

INSIDE THE MIND - EXPLORING ANXIETY DISORDERS

To be diagnosed with GAD, individuals must meet specific criteria outlined in the Diagnostic and Statistical Manual of Mental Disorders (DSM-5). According to the DSM-5, the diagnostic criteria for GAD include the following:

1. Excessive Worrying: The individual experiences persistent and excessive worry about a range of different issues, such as work, health, family, finances, or everyday situations. This worrying occurs more days than not and lasts for at least six months.

2. Difficulty Controlling Worry: The person finds it challenging to control or stop the worrying, even when they recognize that it is excessive or irrational.

3. Physical Symptoms: GAD often manifests with physical symptoms, such as restlessness, fatigue, muscle tension, irritability, difficulty concentrating, and sleep disturbances.

4. Impairment in Daily Life: The excessive worrying and associated symptoms signi cantly interfere with the person's ability to function in various areas of their life, including work, social relationships, and personal well-being.

5. Absence of Other Factors: The symptoms cannot be attributed to the physiological effects of a substance or another medical condition, and they cannot be better explained by another mental disorder.

It is important to note that meeting these criteria alone does not necessarily indicate the presence of GAD. A professional evaluation by a quali ed healthcare provider, such as a psychiatrist or psychologist, is essential to make an accurate diagnosis. They will consider the duration, intensity, and impact of the symptoms, as well as rule out other possible causes.

Inside the Mind: Exploring A - Z of Anxiety Disorders

Understanding the diagnostic criteria for GAD can help individuals recognize when their worry and anxiety may be crossing into a more signi cant problem. If you or someone you know is experiencing persistent and excessive worrying that is interfering with daily life, seeking professional help is crucial. Early intervention and appropriate treatment can signi cantly improve the quality of life for those living with GAD.

In the next subchapter, we will explore the treatment options available for individuals diagnosed with GAD, providing insights into therapy, medication, and self-help strategies that can effectively manage this disorder.

Treatment Options for GAD## Treatment Options for GAD

Inside the Mind: Exploring Anxiety Disorders

Generalized Anxiety Disorder (GAD) is a common mental health condition that affects millions of people worldwide. If you or someone you know is struggling with GAD, it is important to understand that there are effective treatment options available. In this subchapter, we will explore the various treatment approaches for GAD to help you navigate your way towards a happier and healthier life.

1. Psychotherapy: One of the most common and effectivetreatments for GAD is psychotherapy. This form of therapy involves talking to a mental health

professional who can help you identify and manage the underlying causes of your anxiety. Cognitive Behavioral Therapy (CBT) is a widely used approach that focuses on changing negative thought patterns and behaviors. It can help you develop coping strategies and improve your overall well-being.

2. Medication: In some cases, medication may be prescribedto manage the symptoms of GAD. Antidepressants, such as selective serotonin reuptake inhibitors (SSRIs), and benzodiazepines are commonly prescribed to reduce anxiety levels. It is crucial to work closely with a healthcare provider to nd the right medication and dosage for your individual needs.

3. Lifestyle Changes: Making certain lifestyle changes can alsobe bene cial in managing GAD. Regular exercise, a balanced diet, and suf cient sleep can signi cantly improve your mental health. Avoiding caffeine and alcohol can also help reduce anxiety symptoms. Additionally, stress management techniques such as mindfulness, yoga, and deep breathing exercises can provide relief from anxiety.

INSIDE THE MIND - EXPLORING ANXIETY DISORDERS

4. Support Groups: Joining a support group for individuals with anxiety disorders can provide a sense of community and understanding. Sharing experiences and coping strategies with others who are going through similar challenges can be incredibly empowering and comforting. Support groups can be found locally or online, making it easier to connect with others.

5. Alternative Therapies: Some individuals nd relief from GAD symptoms through alternative therapies such as acupuncture, massage, or herbal supplements. While these approaches may not have scienti c evidence to support their effectiveness, they can be worth exploring if they resonate with you.

Remember, treatment for GAD is not one-size- ts-all, and what works for one person may not work for another. It is essential to consult with a healthcare professional to determine the best course of action for your speci c needs. With the right combination of therapies and support, managing GAD is possible, and you can lead a ful lling life free from excessive worry and anxiety.

Chapter 3 Panic Disorder

Overview of Panic Disorder

Chapter 3: Panic Disorder

Overview of Panic Disorder

Inside the Mind: Exploring A - Z of Anxiety Disorders

Panic disorder is one of the most common anxiety disorders that affects millions of people around the world. It is characterized by recurring and unexpected panic attacks, which are intense periods of fear and discomfort that can last for several minutes. These panic attacks can be extremely distressing and may cause individuals to feel like they are losing control or even dying. Understanding the basics of panic disorder is crucial in order to recognize its symptoms and seek appropriate help.

One of the key features of panic disorder is the presence of sudden and repeated panic attacks. These attacks can occur without any apparent trigger or can be triggered by certain situations or objects, such as crowded places or heights. During a panic attack, individuals may experience a combination of physical symptoms, including rapid heartbeat, sweating, trembling, shortness of breath, chest pain, dizziness, and a sense of impending doom.

The fear of having another panic attack can lead to signi cant changes in behavior. People with panic disorder often develop agoraphobia, which is the fear of being in places or situations where escape might be dif cult or embarrassing, or where help may not be readily available. As a result, they may avoid certain places or situations, such as crowded places, public transportation, or even leaving their homes altogether.

The exact cause of panic disorder is not fully understood, but research suggests that it is a complex interplay of genetic, biological, and environmental factors. It is believed that imbalances in brain chemicals, such as serotonin and norepinephrine, play a role in the development of panic disorder. Additionally, individuals with a family history of anxiety disorders are more likely to develop panic disorder themselves.

Inside the Mind: Exploring Anxiety Disorders

Fortunately, panic disorder is a highly treatable condition. Various treatment options are available, including psychotherapy and medication. Cognitive-behavioral therapy

(CBT) is often recommended as the rst-line treatment for panic disorder. This therapy helps individuals identify and challenge their negative thoughts and beliefs, and teaches them coping strategies to manage their anxiety. Medications such as selective serotonin reuptake inhibitors (SSRIs) and benzodiazepines may also be prescribed to help alleviate symptoms.

It is important to remember that seeking help is essential for managing panic disorder. With the right treatment and support, individuals with panic disorder can regain control of their lives and reduce the impact of panic attacks on their daily functioning. If you or someone you know is experiencing symptoms of panic disorder, it is always advisable to consult a healthcare professional for an accurate diagnosis and appropriate treatment options.

Causes and Risk Factors of Panic Disorder

Causes and Risk Factors of Panic Disorder

Understanding the causes and risk factors associated with panic disorder is essential in comprehending this anxiety disorder. Panic disorder is characterized by recurring and unexpected panic attacks, which are intense episodes of fear and anxiety. These attacks are often accompanied by physical symptoms such as rapid heart rate, shortness of breath, trembling, and a feeling of impending doom. While panic disorder can occur in anyone, regardless of age or background, certain factors may increase the likelihood of developing this condition.

Inside the Mind: Exploring A - Z of Anxiety Disorders

One of the primary causes of panic disorder is believed to be a combination of genetic and environmental factors. Research suggests that individuals with a family history of panic disorder or other anxiety disorders are more susceptible to developing this condition. Additionally, traumatic life events, such as the loss of a loved one, physical or emotional abuse, or a major life transition, can trigger the onset of panic disorder.

Neurochemical imbalances in the brain also play a role in the development of panic disorder. Studies have shown that individuals with panic disorder may have abnormalities in the way their brains regulate the neurotransmitter serotonin, which is involved in mood regulation. This imbalance can contribute to the intense feelings of fear and anxiety experienced during panic attacks.

ANDREW D BEATTIE

Another risk factor for panic disorder is the presence of other mental health conditions. Individuals who already have generalized anxiety disorder, social anxiety disorder, or depression are at a higher risk of developing panic disorder. These conditions often coexist and can exacerbate the symptoms of one another.

Certain personality traits and coping mechanisms may also increase the risk of developing panic disorder. People who are more prone to negative thinking, have a tendency to catastrophize situations, or have a high need for control may be more susceptible to developing panic disorder. Additionally, individuals who have dif culty coping with stress or have a history of childhood adversity may be at a higher risk.

It is important to note that while these factors may increase the likelihood of developing panic disorder, they do not guarantee the development of the condition. Each individual's experience with panic disorder is unique, and it is crucial to consult a healthcare professional for a proper diagnosis and treatment plan.

By understanding the causes and risk factors associated with panic disorder, individuals and their loved ones can be better equipped to recognize the signs and seek appropriate help. Educating oneself about anxiety disorders, such as panic disorder, is a vital step in building empathy and support within the community.

Diagnostic Criteria for Panic Disorder

Diagnostic Criteria for Panic Disorder

Inside the Mind: Exploring A - Z of Anxiety Disorders

Panic disorder is a type of anxiety disorder characterized by the occurrence of unexpected panic attacks, which are intense periods of fear or discomfort that reach their peak within minutes. These panic attacks are often accompanied by physical symptoms such as rapid heartbeat, shortness of breath, dizziness, trembling, and a sense of impending doom. If you or someone you know is experiencing these symptoms, it is important to understand the diagnostic criteria for panic disorder.

The Diagnostic and Statistical Manual of Mental Disorders (DSM-5) provides a set of criteria used by mental health professionals to diagnose panic disorder. To be diagnosed with panic disorder, an individual must meet the following criteria:

1. Recurrent panic attacks: The person experiencesunexpected panic attacks on a regular basis, and at least one of the attacks has been followed by at least one month of persistent worry about having additional attacks or their consequences, such as going crazy or having a heart attack.

2. Apprehension about future attacks: The person isconstantly worried about having more panic attacks, and this worry signi cantly affects their daily life and functioning.

3. Behavioral changes: The person may develop avoidancebehaviors, such as avoiding certain situations or places where panic attacks have occurred in the past, in an attempt to prevent future attacks.

4. Exclusion of other medical conditions: The panic attacksare not caused by the direct effects of a substance or a medical condition, such as a hyperthyroidism or a heart condition.

It is important to note that panic attacks can also occur in other anxiety disorders or as a result of certain medical conditions. Therefore, a thorough assessment by a quali ed mental health professional is crucial to determine a correct diagnosis.

Understanding the diagnostic criteria for panic disorder can help individuals and their loved ones seek appropriate treatment and support. Treatment options for panic disorder may include cognitive-behavioral therapy (CBT), medication, or a combination of both. CBT aims to help individuals identify and change negative thought patterns and behaviors that contribute to panic attacks. Medications such as selective serotonin reuptake inhibitors (SSRIs) or benzodiazepines may also be prescribed to help manage the symptoms.

By familiarizing ourselves with the diagnostic criteria for panic disorder, we can promote awareness and reduce the stigma surrounding anxiety disorders. Remember, seeking professional help is essential for an accurate diagnosis and effective treatment.

Treatment Options for Panic Disorder

Treatment Options for Panic Disorder

Panic disorder is a type of anxiety disorder characterized by recurring panic attacks, which are sudden episodes of intense fear and physical symptoms such as a racing heart, shortness of breath, and dizziness. If you or someone you know is experiencing panic attacks, it is important to seek help and explore treatment options that can alleviate the symptoms and improve overall well-being. In this subchapter, we will discuss the various treatment options available for panic disorder.

1. Psychotherapy: One of the most effective treatments forpanic disorder is psychotherapy. Cognitive-behavioral therapy (CBT) is commonly used to help individuals identify and change negative thought patterns and behaviors that contribute to panic attacks. This therapy equips individuals with coping mechanisms and relaxation techniques to manage panic symptoms.

2. Medication: In some cases, medication may be prescribedto help control panic attacks and reduce anxiety. Selective serotonin reuptake inhibitors (SSRIs) and benzodiazepines are commonly prescribed medications for panic disorder. It is important to consult with a healthcare provider to determine the most suitable medication and dosage for your speci c needs.

3. Lifestyle modi cations: Making certain lifestyle changescan greatly improve the management of panic

disorder. Regular exercise, adequate sleep, and a healthy diet can help reduce anxiety levels. Avoiding caffeine, alcohol, and nicotine is also recommended, as these substances can trigger panic attacks.

4. Stress management techniques: Learning stressmanagement techniques, such as deep breathing exercises, meditation, and mindfulness, can help individuals with panic disorder better cope with stress and prevent panic attacks. These techniques promote relaxation and reduce anxiety levels.

5. Support groups: Joining a support group can provide asense of community and understanding for individuals with panic disorder. Sharing experiences and receiving support from others who have gone through similar situations can be bene cial in managing panic attacks.

Remember, everyone's journey with panic disorder is unique, and treatment options may vary depending on individual needs. It is important to consult with a healthcare professional to develop a personalized treatment plan. With the right support and treatment, individuals with panic disorder can regain control over their lives and experience a signi cant reduction in panic attacks and anxiety levels.

Chapter 4: Social Anxiety Disorder (SAD)

Overview of Social Anxiety Disorder

Inside the Mind: Exploring A - Z of Anxiety Disorders

Inside the Mind: Exploring Anxiety Disorders

Social Anxiety Disorder, also known as social phobia, is a
common anxiety disorder that affects many individuals around

the world. It is characterized by an intense fear of social situations, particularly those involving interactions with others. People with social anxiety disorder often feel extremely self-conscious, worried about being judged or embarrassed, and may avoid social situations altogether. This subchapter aims to provide a comprehensive overview of social anxiety disorder, its symptoms, causes, and available treatment options.

Symptoms of social anxiety disorder can vary from person to person, but common signs include excessive sweating, trembling, rapid heartbeat, nausea, and dif culty speaking. These physical symptoms are often accompanied by intense feelings of fear, anxiety, and a strong desire to escape or avoid the situation altogether. It is important to note that social anxiety disorder is more than just shyness or occasional nervousness in social situations. It signi cantly impacts an individual's daily life, relationships, and overall well-being.

Inside the Mind: Exploring Anxiety Disorders

The exact cause of social anxiety disorder is not yet fully understood, but researchers believe that a combination of genetic, environmental, and psychological factors contribute to its development. Some individuals may have a genetic predisposition to anxiety disorders, while others may have experienced traumatic or embarrassing social situations in the past. Additionally, individuals with low self-esteem or a history of other anxiety disorders may be more prone to developing social anxiety disorder.

Fortunately, social anxiety disorder is a treatable condition, and there are several effective treatment options available. Cognitive-behavioral therapy (CBT) is often recommended, which helps individuals identify and challenge negative thought patterns and beliefs that contribute to their anxiety. In some cases, medication such as selective serotonin reuptake inhibitors (SSRIs) may be prescribed to help manage symptoms. Additionally, self-help strategies such as practicing relaxation techniques, engaging in regular exercise, and gradually exposing oneself to feared social situations can also be bene cial.

Inside the Mind: Exploring Anxiety Disorders

Causes and Risk Factors of SAD

It is important to seek professional help if you suspect you or someone you know may be suffering from social anxiety disorder. With the right support, individuals with social anxiety disorder can learn to manage their symptoms, improve their con dence, and lead ful lling lives. This subchapter is just the beginning of understanding social anxiety disorder, and further exploration of other anxiety disorders will be covered in the subsequent chapters of this book.

Causes and Risk Factors of SAD

Social Anxiety Disorder (SAD), also known as social phobia, is a common anxiety disorder that affects millions of people worldwide. It is characterized by an intense fear of social situations, leading individuals to avoid or feel extremely anxious in social interactions. While the exact cause of SAD is unknown, research suggests that a combination of genetic, environmental, and psychological factors contribute to its development.

One of the primary causes of SAD is believed to be genetics. Studies have shown that individuals with a family history of anxiety disorders are more likely to develop SAD themselves. This suggests that certain genes may play a role in predisposing individuals to this disorder. However, it is important to note that genetics alone cannot fully explain the development of SAD, and other factors must also be considered.

Environmental factors can also contribute to the development of SAD. Traumatic experiences, such as bullying or humiliation in social situations, can leave a lasting impact and increase the risk of developing social anxiety. Additionally, growing up in an overly critical or overprotective environment can also contribute to the development of SAD. These environmental factors can shape an individual's beliefs and perceptions about social interactions, leading to the development of anxiety.

Inside the Mind: Exploring A - Z of Anxiety Disorders

Psychological factors also play a signi cant role in the development of SAD. Low self-esteem, negative selfperception, and a fear of judgment or rejection can contribute to the onset of social anxiety. Individuals with SAD often have irrational thoughts and beliefs about social situations, leading them to anticipate negative outcomes and feel anxious or uncomfortable in these settings.

Other risk factors that may increase the likelihood of developing SAD include a history of shyness or behavioral inhibition in childhood, a history of other anxiety disorders, and substance abuse. Additionally, certain personality traits, such as being introverted or having a sensitive temperament, may also increase the risk of developing social anxiety.

It is important to understand that SAD is a complex disorder with multiple causes and risk factors. The interplay between genetics, environment, and psychological factors can vary from person to person. Recognizing these factors can help individuals and their loved ones better understand the nature of SAD and seek appropriate treatment and support.

If you or someone you know is struggling with social anxiety, it is important to reach out for help. Effective treatments, such as cognitive-behavioral therapy and medication, can signi cantly reduce the symptoms of SAD and improve quality of life. Remember, you are not alone, and there is support available to help you navigate the challenges of social anxiety disorder.

Diagnostic Criteria for SAD**Diagnostic**

Criteria for SAD

Social Anxiety Disorder (SAD), also known as social phobia, is a common anxiety disorder that affects millions of people worldwide. It is characterized by an intense fear or anxiety in social situations, leading to avoidance of such situations and signi cant distress in daily life. In this subchapter, we will explore the diagnostic criteria for SAD, helping you understand and recognize the signs and symptoms of this disorder.

The Diagnostic and Statistical Manual of Mental Disorders (DSM-5), which is widely used by mental health professionals, provides speci c criteria for diagnosing SAD. To be diagnosed with SAD, an individual must meet the following criteria:

1. Persistent fear or anxiety: The person experiences apersistent and excessive fear or anxiety in one or more social situations where they may be exposed to possible scrutiny by others. This fear is out of proportion to the actual threat posed by the situation.

2. Avoidance behaviors: The individual actively avoids orendures these social situations with intense fear or anxiety. This may include avoiding parties, public speaking, or even everyday interactions like eating in public.

3. Interference with daily life: The fear, anxiety, or avoidancebehaviors signi cantly interfere with the person's daily routine, occupation, academic functioning, or social activities. It may cause distress

and impair their ability to form relationships or pursue their goals.

4. Duration: The fear, anxiety, or avoidance behaviors persistfor six months or longer.
5. Not attributable to other factors: The symptoms are notbetter explained by another mental disorder, such as panic disorder, body dysmorphic disorder, or autism spectrum disorder.

It's important to note that experiencing occasional nervousness or anxiety in social situations is normal. However, for individuals with SAD, the fear and anxiety are persistent, overwhelming, and interfere with their ability to function in social settings.

If you or someone you know meets the criteria for SAD, it is crucial to seek professional help. Effective treatments, including cognitive-behavioral therapy and medication, can signi cantly reduce symptoms and improve the quality of life.

Understanding the diagnostic criteria for SAD is a crucial step in recognizing and addressing the disorder. By increasing awareness and knowledge, we can work together to support those affected by SAD and create a more inclusive and understanding society.

Treatment Options for SAD## Treatment Options for SAD

Social Anxiety Disorder (SAD) is a common anxiety disorder that affects millions of people worldwide. It is characterized by an intense fear of social situations and the fear of being judged or embarrassed by others. Fortunately, there are several effective treatment options available for individuals suffering from SAD.

One of the most common and successful treatments for SAD is cognitive-behavioral therapy (CBT). CBT aims to identify and change negative thought patterns and behaviors that contribute to social anxiety. Through therapy sessions, individuals learn to challenge their irrational beliefs, develop more realistic thoughts, and gradually expose themselves to anxiety-provoking situations. CBT equips individuals with valuable coping mechanisms, helping them manage their anxiety and improve their social interactions.

Medication can also be a helpful treatment option for individuals with SAD. Selective serotonin reuptake inhibitors (SSRIs) are the most commonly prescribed medications for anxiety disorders. These medications work by increasing the levels of serotonin in the brain, which helps regulate mood and anxiety. While medication can be effective in reducing symptoms of SAD, it is often combined with therapy for the best results.

In addition to therapy and medication, lifestyle changes can greatly improve the symptoms of SAD. Regular exercise has been shown to reduce anxiety and improve overall mental well-being. Engaging in physical activity also provides an opportunity for individuals to face their fears and gradually build con dence in social situations.

Support groups and self-help resources can also be bene cial for individuals with SAD. Joining a support group allows individuals to connect with others who understand their struggles and share coping strategies. Self-help books, online resources, and mobile applications can provide valuable information and techniques for managing social anxiety.

It is essential for individuals with SAD to seek professional help and not suffer in silence. A quali ed mental health professional can provide an accurate diagnosis and recommend the most suitable treatment option. Remember, treatment for SAD is highly effective, and with the right support, individuals can overcome their fears and lead ful lling lives.

In conclusion, there are various treatment options available for individuals with SAD. Cognitive-behavioral therapy, medication, lifestyle changes, and support resources can all contribute to reducing social anxiety symptoms. It is crucial for individuals to reach out for help and explore these treatment options to regain control over their lives. With the right treatment and support, individuals with SAD can conquer their fears and thrive in social situations.

Chapter 5: Obsessive-Compulsive Disorder (OCD)

Overview of Obsessive-Compulsive Disorder

Obsessive-Compulsive Disorder (OCD) is a mental health condition that affects millions of people worldwide. It is characterized by recurring thoughts, images, or urges (obsessions) that cause anxiety and repetitive behaviors or mental acts (compulsions) performed to alleviate that anxiety. OCD can be a debilitating condition, often interfering with daily life and causing signi cant distress.

Obsessions are intrusive and unwanted thoughts, images, or urges that are dif cult to control. They can range from fears of contamination, doubts about safety, or a need for symmetry and order. These obsessions often cause intense anxiety and distress, leading individuals to engage in compulsive behaviors to try and alleviate their fears.

Compulsions, on the other hand, are repetitive behaviors or mental acts that individuals with OCD feel compelled to perform. Common compulsions include excessive hand washing, checking locks or appliances, counting, or repeating words or phrases. These compulsions temporarily relieve anxiety but are often time-consuming and can interfere with daily life.

OCD is a chronic condition that typically develops in late adolescence or early adulthood, although it can start in childhood as well. The exact cause of OCD is unknown, but it is believed to be a combination of genetic, environmental, and neurological factors. Certain life events, such as trauma or stress, can also trigger or exacerbate symptoms.

Living with OCD can be challenging, but effective treatments are available. Cognitive-Behavioral Therapy (CBT) is the gold standard treatment for OCD. It involves exposure and response prevention, which helps individuals confront their fears and reduce the need to engage in compulsive behaviors. Medications, such as selective serotonin reuptake inhibitors (SSRIs), may also be prescribed to manage symptoms.

It is crucial to understand that OCD is not simply a quirk or personality trait. It is a legitimate medical condition that requires empathy, support, and appropriate treatment. Unfortunately, there are still misconceptions and stigmas surrounding OCD, which can prevent individuals from seeking help.

If you or someone you know is struggling with OCD, it is essential to reach out for professional help. OCD is a treatable condition, and with the right support, individuals can learn to manage their symptoms and lead ful lling lives.

In the upcoming chapters of "Inside the Mind: Exploring A - Z of Anxiety Disorders," we will delve deeper into the various aspects of OCD, including its impact on relationships, work, and daily functioning. We will also explore other anxiety disorders to provide a comprehensive understanding of these conditions and promote awareness and understanding among the general public.

Causes and Risk Factors of OCDCauses and Risk Factors of OCD

Obsessive-Compulsive Disorder (OCD) is a complex anxiety disorder that affects millions of people worldwide.

Understanding the causes and risk factors associated with OCD can help shed light on this debilitating condition. In this subchapter, we will explore the various factors that contribute to the development of OCD.

The exact cause of OCD is still not fully understood. However, researchers believe that a combination of genetic, environmental, and neurobiological factors play a role in its onset. Studies have shown that individuals with a family history of OCD are more likely to develop the disorder, indicating a genetic predisposition. It is thought that certain genes may affect the brain's functioning, leading to an imbalance in neurotransmitters like serotonin, which is associated with mood regulation.

Environmental factors can also contribute to the development of OCD. Traumatic events, such as physical or sexual abuse, can trigger the onset of OCD symptoms. Additionally, stressful life events, such as the loss of a loved one or a major life transition, can exacerbate existing OCD symptoms or contribute to their development.

Neurobiological factors are believed to play a signi cant role in OCD. The brain regions responsible for decision-making, impulse control, and habit formation, such as the orbitofrontal cortex, anterior cingulate cortex, and basal ganglia, have been found to be hyperactive in individuals with OCD. This hyperactivity leads to the intrusive thoughts and repetitive behaviors characteristic of the disorder.

Furthermore, certain personality traits and cognitive factors may increase the risk of developing OCD. Perfectionism, for example, can contribute to obsessive thoughts and the need for excessive orderliness. Some individuals with OCD also have a tendency to overestimate the likelihood of harm or danger, leading to excessive anxiety and the need to engage in compulsive behaviors to alleviate these fears.

It is essential to note that while these factors can increase the risk of developing OCD, they do not guarantee the development of the disorder. OCD is a complex condition with multiple contributing factors, and each individual's experience with the disorder is unique.

By understanding the causes and risk factors of OCD, we can promote greater awareness and empathy towards those affected by the disorder. This knowledge also highlights the importance of early intervention and appropriate treatment options to help individuals manage their symptoms and improve their quality of life.

Diagnostic Criteria for OCDDiagnostic Criteria for OCD

Obsessive-Compulsive Disorder (OCD) is a mental health condition that affects millions of people worldwide. It is characterized by the presence of persistent, intrusive thoughts (obsessions) and repetitive, ritualistic behaviors (compulsions). In order to diagnose OCD, mental health professionals follow speci c diagnostic criteria outlined in the Diagnostic and Statistical Manual of Mental Disorders (DSM-5).

According to the DSM-5, there are several key criteria that must be met for an individual to be diagnosed with OCD. First and foremost, the person must experience either obsessions or compulsions, or both. Obsessions are intrusive thoughts, urges, or images that are unwanted and cause signi cant distress. Compulsions, on the other hand, are repetitive behaviors or mental acts that the person feels driven to perform in response to their obsessions.

In addition to the presence of obsessions and/or compulsions, the individual must also recognize that these thoughts and behaviors are excessive or unreasonable. They may try to resist or ignore them, but ultimately feel compelled to engage in the rituals to alleviate anxiety or prevent a feared event. These obsessions and compulsions are time-consuming, taking up at least one hour per day, and interfere with the person's daily functioning or cause signi cant distress.

Furthermore, the obsessions and compulsions must not be better explained by another mental disorder. Sometimes, symptoms of OCD can overlap with other anxiety disorders or conditions such as body dysmorphic disorder or hoarding disorder. It is important for mental health professionals to rule out these possibilities and ensure that the symptoms align with the diagnostic criteria for OCD.

Finally, it is crucial to note that OCD can manifest in various ways and can center around different themes. Some common obsessions include fears of contamination, doubting, the need for symmetry, or aggressive impulses. Compulsions may involve excessive cleaning, checking, counting, or arranging objects. However, these are just a few examples, and OCD can present in countless other forms.

Understanding the diagnostic criteria for OCD can help individuals recognize when they may be experiencing symptoms of this disorder. If you or someone you know is struggling with persistent intrusive thoughts and repetitive behaviors that interfere with daily life, it is essential to seek professional help. With proper diagnosis and treatment, individuals with OCD can manage their symptoms and improve their overall quality of life.

Treatment Options for OCD## Treatment Options for OCD

Obsessive-Compulsive Disorder (OCD) is a debilitating anxiety disorder that affects millions of people worldwide. If you or someone you know is struggling with OCD, it is important to understand that there are effective treatment options available to help manage and alleviate the symptoms. In this chapter, we will explore the various treatment options for OCD, providing insights into the A-Z of Anxiety Disorders.

1. Cognitive-Behavioral Therapy (CBT): CBT is considered the gold standard treatment for OCD. It focuses on identifying and challenging obsessive thoughts while helping individuals develop healthier coping mechanisms. CBT often incorporates exposure and response prevention (ERP), which gradually exposes individuals to their fears and prevents the accompanying compulsions. Through therapy sessions, individuals can learn to reframe their thoughts and break free from the cycle of obsessions and compulsions.

Inside the Mind: Exploring A - Z of Anxiety Disorders

INSIDE THE MIND - EXPLORING ANXIETY DISORDERS

2. Medication: In some cases, medication may be prescribed to assist in managing OCD symptoms. Selective serotonin reuptake inhibitors (SSRIs) are commonly used antidepressants that have shown effectiveness in reducing OCD symptoms. It is important to consult with a psychiatrist or healthcare professional to determine the appropriate medication and dosage.

3. Support Groups: Joining a support group can provide individuals with a sense of community and understanding. Sharing experiences, discussing coping strategies, and receiving encouragement from others who have faced similar challenges can be highly bene cial. Support groups can be found both online and in-person, allowing individuals to connect with others who have an A-Z of Anxiety Disorders.

1. Lifestyle Changes: Engaging in healthy lifestyle practicescan also aid in managing OCD symptoms. Regular exercise, maintaining a balanced diet, getting suf cient sleep, and practicing relaxation techniques like meditation or deep breathing exercises can contribute to overall well-being and help reduce anxiety levels.

2. Alternative Therapies: Some individuals may nd relieffrom symptoms through alternative therapies such as acupuncture, yoga, or mindfulness meditation. While these approaches may not be suitable for everyone, they can be valuable adjuncts to traditional treatments.

Remember, everyone's journey with OCD is unique, and nding the right treatment approach may require trial and error. It is crucial to have a supportive network and consult with mental health professionals who specialize in anxiety disorders. With the right treatment, support, and a comprehensive understanding of the A-Z of Anxiety Disorders, individuals with OCD can regain control over their lives and experience a signi cant improvement in their quality of life.

Chapter 6: Post-Traumatic Stress Disorder (PTSD)

Overview of Post-Traumatic Stress Disorder

Chapter 6: Post-Traumatic Stress Disorder (PTSD)

Overview of Post-Traumatic Stress Disorder

Post-Traumatic Stress Disorder (PTSD) is a mental health condition that can develop in individuals who have experienced or witnessed a traumatic event. It can affect people from all walks of life, regardless of age, gender, or background. In this subchapter, we will delve into the intricacies of PTSD, exploring its causes, symptoms, and available treatment options.

PTSD is often associated with individuals who have been exposed to war zones or other extreme situations, but it can also arise from other traumatic experiences, such as natural disasters, accidents, physical or sexual assault, or the sudden loss of a loved one. The disorder can manifest itself immediately after the event or even months or years later. It affects the sufferer's ability to function in their daily lives, as they may experience intense and recurring ashbacks, nightmares, and intrusive thoughts related to the traumatic event.

One of the key symptoms of PTSD is hyperarousal, where the individual remains in a constant state of vigilance, always on edge, and easily startled. This heightened state of anxiety can lead to dif culties in concentration, irritability, and even issues with sleep. Avoidance behaviors are also common, as individuals may try to steer clear of reminders or situations that trigger their traumatic memories. They may isolate themselves from others, lose interest in activities they once enjoyed, or develop negative emotions like guilt, shame, or anger.

Recognizing the signs and symptoms of PTSD is crucial for early intervention and treatment. While it is a serious and potentially debilitating mental health condition, there are effective treatments available. Psychotherapy, especially cognitive-behavioral therapy (CBT), has shown promising results in helping individuals manage their symptoms and regain control over their lives. Medications, such as selective serotonin reuptake inhibitors (SSRIs), can also be prescribed to alleviate the symptoms of anxiety and depression commonly associated with PTSD.

It is important to understand that seeking help and support is not a sign of weakness but rather a courageous step towards healing. Friends, family, and support groups can provide a vital network of understanding and empathy for individuals with PTSD. Education and awareness about PTSD are crucial to break the stigma surrounding mental health and create a more compassionate and inclusive society.

In conclusion, PTSD is a complex mental health disorder that can affect anyone who has experienced a traumatic event. It can have a profound impact on the individual's emotional well-being, relationships, and overall quality of life. However, with early intervention and appropriate treatment, individuals with PTSD can nd relief from their symptoms and regain control over their lives.

Causes and Risk Factors of PTSD
Causes and Risk Factors of PTSD

Post-traumatic stress disorder (PTSD) is a debilitating mental health condition that can develop after experiencing or witnessing a traumatic event. It affects millions of people worldwide, and understanding its causes and risk factors is crucial for both individuals who may be suffering from it and the general public. This subchapter aims to delve into the various factors that contribute to the development of PTSD, shedding light on its complex nature.

Traumatic events are the primary trigger for PTSD. These events can vary widely, ranging from natural disasters and accidents to physical or sexual assault, combat exposure, or witnessing acts of violence. The intensity and duration of the trauma play a signi cant role in the likelihood of developing PTSD. However, it's important to note that not everyone exposed to traumatic events will develop the disorder.

Several risk factors increase a person's susceptibility to developing PTSD. One such factor is a history of previous trauma or adverse experiences, which can make individuals more vulnerable to the effects of subsequent traumatic events.

Additionally, a lack of a strong support system, such as family or friends, can increase the risk of developing PTSD.

Biological factors also contribute to the development of PTSD. Research has shown that individuals with a family history of anxiety disorders or depression may be genetically predisposed to develop the disorder. Moreover, differences in brain structure and function, speci cally in the areas associated with fear and stress responses, have been observed in individuals with PTSD.

Psychological factors, such as pre-existing mental health conditions, can heighten the risk of developing PTSD. Conditions like depression, anxiety disorders, or substance abuse disorders can make individuals more susceptible to experiencing traumatic events and developing PTSD as a result.

Social factors, including socio-economic status, cultural background, and access to resources, can also in uence the likelihood of developing PTSD. Individuals from marginalized communities or those living in poverty may face additional challenges in terms of trauma exposure and access to adequate support and treatment.

Understanding the causes and risk factors of PTSD is vital for the general public. By increasing awareness, we can reduce the stigma surrounding mental health conditions and provide support to those in need. It is crucial to promote a compassionate and empathetic society that recognizes the impact of trauma and works towards creating a safe and inclusive environment for all individuals.

Diagnostic Criteria for PTSD## Diagnostic Criteria for PTSD

Post-Traumatic Stress Disorder (PTSD) is a psychiatric disorder that can occur in individuals who have experienced or witnessed a traumatic event. It can manifest in a range of symptoms that severely impact a person's daily life. In this subchapter, we will explore the diagnostic criteria for PTSD, helping you understand the signs and symptoms associated with this anxiety disorder.

To receive a diagnosis of PTSD, one must have experienced a traumatic event. This can include but is not limited to, physical or sexual assault, natural disasters, serious accidents, or military combat. The traumatic event must be distressing and outside the realm of typical human experience.

The diagnostic criteria for PTSD are divided into four main categories: intrusion symptoms, avoidance symptoms, negative alterations in cognition and mood, and alterations in arousal and reactivity. Let's delve into each category:

1. Intrusion symptoms: These involve the persistent reexperiencing of the traumatic event. This can include distressing memories, ashbacks, nightmares, or intense psychological or physiological reactions triggered by reminders of the event.
2. Avoidance symptoms: Individuals with PTSD often

try toavoid anything that reminds them of the traumatic event. This can involve avoiding certain places, people, activities, or even conversations related to the event.

3. Negative alterations in cognition and mood: PTSD can leadto negative thoughts and feelings associated with the traumatic event. These may include distorted beliefs about oneself or others, persistent negative emotions, feelings of detachment, or a diminished interest in activities previously enjoyed.

4. Alterations in arousal and reactivity: People with PTSD mayexhibit changes in their behavior and physical reactions. This can include irritability, dif culty sleeping, hypervigilance, exaggerated startle responses, or reckless or self-destructive behavior.

To receive a formal diagnosis of PTSD, symptoms must persist for at least one month and signi cantly impair the individual's ability to function in daily life. It is essential to note that everyone's experience with PTSD is unique, and the severity and duration of symptoms can vary.

If you or someone you know is experiencing symptoms that align with the diagnostic criteria for PTSD, it is crucial to seek professional help. Treatment options, such as therapy and medication, can effectively alleviate symptoms and promote healing.

Understanding the diagnostic criteria for PTSD can help you recognize and empathize with individuals who may be suffering silently. By increasing awareness and knowledge of this anxiety disorder, we can better support those affected and foster a more compassionate society.

Treatment Options for PTSD## Treatment Options for PTSD

Post-Traumatic Stress Disorder (PTSD) is a debilitating anxiety disorder that often occurs after experiencing or witnessing a traumatic event. It can have a profound impact on an individual's mental and emotional well-being, but there is hope. This subchapter explores the various treatment options available for individuals struggling with PTSD.

One of the most effective treatments for PTSD is psychotherapy. This form of therapy allows individuals to talk about their experiences and emotions in a safe and supportive environment. Cognitive Behavioral Therapy (CBT) is a speci c type of psychotherapy commonly used for PTSD. It focuses on identifying and changing negative thought patterns and behaviors that contribute to distressing symptoms. Through CBT, individuals can learn coping strategies to manage their anxiety and regain control over their lives.

Eye Movement Desensitization and Reprocessing (EMDR) is another therapy option for PTSD. This innovative treatment involves the use of bilateral stimulation, such as eye movements or taps, while recalling traumatic memories. EMDR helps individuals process their traumatic experiences and reduce the distress associated with them. It can be particularly bene cial for those who struggle with intrusive thoughts or nightmares related to their trauma.

Inside the Mind: Exploring A - Z of Anxiety Disorders

INSIDE THE MIND - EXPLORING ANXIETY DISORDERS

Inside the Mind: Exploring Anxiety Disorders

Medication can also play a role in treating PTSD. Antidepressants, such as selective serotonin reuptake inhibitors (SSRIs), can help reduce symptoms of anxiety and depression commonly associated with PTSD. These medications work by balancing brain chemicals and can provide relief for many individuals. It is important to consult with a healthcare professional to determine the most suitable medication and dosage for each individual's speci c needs.

In addition to these traditional treatment options, alternative therapies have shown promise in relieving PTSD symptoms. Mindfulness practices, such as meditation and yoga, can help individuals become more present and grounded, reducing the impact of traumatic memories. Animal-assisted therapy, where individuals interact with trained animals, has also been found to provide comfort and support during the healing process.

It is crucial to remember that everyone's journey with PTSD is unique, and what works for one person may not work for another. Finding the right treatment approach often requires a combination of therapies tailored to individual needs. The road to recovery may be challenging, but with the support of mental health professionals, loved ones, and a commitment to self-care, individuals can reclaim their lives from the grip of PTSD.

If you or someone you know is struggling with PTSD, reach out to a mental health professional who can guide you towards effective treatment options. Remember, healing is possible, and a brighter future awaits.

Chapter 7 Phobias

Overview of Phobias

Chapter 7: Phobias Overview of Phobias

Phobias are a common type of anxiety disorder that affects millions of people worldwide. In this chapter, we will explore the A-Z of anxiety disorders, with a speci c focus on phobias. This overview aims to provide general knowledge and understanding about phobias for the general public.

Phobias are intense and irrational fears of speci c objects, situations, or activities. They can range from common fears such as heights, spiders, or ying, to more unusual fears like clowns or buttons. These fears are often so severe that they can interfere with a person's daily life and cause signi cant distress.

INSIDE THE MIND - EXPLORING ANXIETY DISORDERS

One of the key characteristics of phobias is the extreme avoidance behavior individuals engage in to prevent contact with the feared object or situation. This avoidance can lead to social isolation and limitations in various aspects of life, including work, relationships, and personal growth.

There are three main types of phobias: speci c phobias, social phobia (also known as social anxiety disorder), and agoraphobia. Speci c phobias involve a fear of a particular object or situation, such as dogs or ying. Social phobia is characterized by an intense fear of social situations, such as public speaking or social interactions. Agoraphobia is the fear of being in situations where escape might be dif cult or embarrassing, such as crowded places or open spaces.

Phobias can develop due to a combination of genetic, environmental, and psychological factors. Traumatic experiences, learned behaviors, and cultural in uences can all contribute to the development of phobias. It is important to note that phobias are not a sign of weakness or character aw; they are legitimate medical conditions that can be effectively treated.

Treatment for phobias often involves therapy, such as cognitive-behavioral therapy (CBT), which helps individuals identify and challenge irrational thoughts and beliefs related to their fears. Exposure therapy is another commonly used technique, where individuals gradually face their fears in a controlled and supportive environment. Medications may also be prescribed to alleviate symptoms and manage anxiety.

Understanding phobias is essential for both individuals experiencing them and those around them. By increasing awareness, we can promote empathy and support for individuals with phobias, reducing the stigma associated with anxiety disorders. Building a compassionate and educated society is crucial in helping people overcome their phobias and live ful lling lives.

In the following chapters, we will delve deeper into speci c phobias, social phobia, agoraphobia, and other anxiety disorders, providing comprehensive information to help individuals gain a better understanding of these conditions and the available treatment options.

Common Types of Phobias

Phobias are one of the most common forms of anxiety disorders that affect millions of people worldwide. These intense and irrational fears can cause signi cant distress and disrupt daily life. In this subchapter, we will explore some of the most common types of phobias that individuals may experience.

1. Speci c Phobias: Speci c phobias are characterized by anintense fear of a particular object, situation, or activity. Some common examples include fear of heights (acrophobia), spiders (arachnophobia), ying (aviophobia), and enclosed spaces (claustrophobia). Individuals with speci c phobias often go to great

lengths to avoid their feared stimulus, which can impact their quality of life.

2. Social Phobia: Social phobia, also known as social anxietydisorder, is characterized by an overwhelming fear of social situations. Individuals with social phobia may experience extreme anxiety when interacting with others, leading to avoidance of social gatherings, public speaking, or even daily activities like eating in front of others. This phobia can signi cantly impact an individual's personal and professional relationships.

Inside the Mind: Exploring A - Z of Anxiety Disorders

3. Agoraphobia: Agoraphobia is the fear of being in situations or places where escape may be dif cult or embarrassing. It often leads to avoidance of crowded places, public transportation, or leaving home altogether. Agoraphobia can be debilitating and severely restrict an individual's ability to engage in daily activities.

4. Claustrophobia: Claustrophobia is an intense fear of being in enclosed or con ned spaces. It can manifest in situations such as being in an elevator, crowded rooms, or even tight-tting clothing. Individuals with claustrophobia may experience panic attacks or extreme anxiety in these situations, leading to avoidance behaviors.

5. Blood-Injection-Injury Phobia: This unique phobia involves an intense fear of blood, injections, or injuries. Individuals with this phobia may experience a strong vasovagal response, which can cause them to faint or experience a drop in blood pressure. This fear can result in avoidance of medical procedures or even routine blood tests.

Understanding the common types of phobias is crucial in recognizing and seeking appropriate help. It is important to note that phobias can be effectively treated through various therapeutic approaches, including cognitive-behavioral therapy (CBT) and exposure therapy. By seeking professional help, individuals can learn to manage their fears and regain control over their lives.

In conclusion, phobias are a prevalent form of anxiety disorders that can signi cantly impact an individual's wellbeing. Speci c phobias, social phobia, agoraphobia, claustrophobia, and blood-injection-injury phobia are some of the most common types. Recognizing these fears and seeking appropriate treatment can empower individuals to overcome their phobias and lead ful lling lives.

Causes and Risk Factors of Phobias

Phobias are intense and irrational fears that can signi cantly impact a person's daily life. While it is common for individuals to experience some level of fear or discomfort in certain situations, phobias take these feelings to an extreme level.

Understanding the causes and risk factors associated with phobias is crucial in managing and overcoming these anxiety disorders.

One of the primary causes of phobias is believed to be a combination of genetic and environmental factors. Research suggests that individuals with a family history of anxiety disorders or phobias may be more prone to developing phobias themselves. This genetic predisposition may make certain individuals more susceptible to developing an exaggerated fear response.

Environmental factors also play a signi cant role in the development of phobias. Traumatic experiences, such as being involved in a car accident or witnessing a traumatic event, can trigger a phobia. For example, a person who experienced a dog attack may develop a fear of dogs (cynophobia). Additionally, phobias can be learned through observation or by hearing about others' negative experiences. Children, in particular, are highly susceptible to developing phobias based on their environment.

Another key risk factor for phobias is a history of anxiety disorders or other mental health conditions. Individuals who have previously experienced anxiety or panic attacks may be more likely to develop phobias. Additionally, individuals with a history of depression or post-traumatic stress disorder (PTSD) may be at a higher risk of developing phobias.

Personality traits can also contribute to the development of phobias. People who tend to be more anxious, sensitive, or have a low tolerance for uncertainty may be more prone to developing phobias. Furthermore, individuals who have a tendency to catastrophize or overestimate the potential dangers in situations may also be at a higher risk.

It is important to note that phobias can develop at any age, from childhood to adulthood. However, most phobias typically arise during childhood and adolescence. Early intervention and treatment are crucial in managing phobias and preventing them from escalating into more severe anxiety disorders.

In conclusion, phobias are complex anxiety disorders that are in uenced by a combination of genetic, environmental, and psychological factors. Understanding the causes and risk factors associated with phobias can help individuals and their loved ones recognize the signs and seek appropriate treatment. By addressing these factors, individuals can take steps towards managing and overcoming their phobias, leading to a better quality of life.

Diagnostic Criteria for Phobias## Diagnostic Criteria for Phobias

Phobias, one of the most common anxiety disorders, affect millions of people worldwide. These disorders are characterized by an intense and irrational fear of speci c objects, situations, or activities. In this subchapter, we will explore the diagnostic criteria for phobias, shedding light on the key indicators used by mental health professionals to identify and classify these conditions.

To diagnose a phobia, mental health professionals typically follow the guidelines outlined in the Diagnostic and Statistical Manual of Mental Disorders (DSM-5). According to the DSM-5, the diagnostic criteria for phobias include:

1. Persistent fear: The individual experiences excessive andunreasonable fear or anxiety triggered by a speci c object, situation, or activity. This fear persists for at least six months and is not proportional to the actual danger posed.
2. Avoidance behavior: The person actively avoids the fearedobject, situation, or activity, or endures it with intense distress or anxiety.
3. Interference with daily life: The fear and avoidancebehavior signi cantly interfere with the person's normal routine, occupational or academic functioning, or social activities. It may also cause signi cant distress.
4. Not attributable to another mental disorder: The phobicsymptoms are not better explained by the presence of another mental disorder, such as panic disorder or obsessivecompulsive disorder.

Phobias can be classi ed into two main types: speci c phobias and social phobias. Speci c phobias involve a fear of speci c objects, such as spiders, heights, or ying. Social phobias, on the other hand, revolve around a fear of social situations or scrutiny by others.

It is important to note that phobias are treatable conditions, and seeking professional help can lead to effective management or even complete resolution of symptoms. Treatment options may include exposure therapy, cognitivebehavioral therapy, and, in some cases, medication.

Understanding the diagnostic criteria for phobias allows individuals to recognize when their fears and anxieties may be crossing the line into a diagnosable condition. If you or someone you know experiences persistent and irrational fears that signi cantly impact daily life, it is essential to consult a mental health professional for evaluation and guidance.

By increasing awareness and understanding of phobias, we can help reduce the stigma associated with anxiety disorders and promote a more empathetic and supportive society for individuals facing these challenges.

Treatment Options for Phobias# Treatment Options for Phobias

Phobias are intense and irrational fears that can signi cantly impact one's quality of life. Fortunately, there are various treatment options available to help individuals overcome their phobias and regain control over their lives. This subchapter will explore some of the most effective treatment options for phobias.

One of the most common and successful treatments for phobias is cognitive-behavioral therapy (CBT). CBT aims to change the negative thought patterns and behaviors associated with phobias. Through exposure therapy, individuals are gradually exposed to the object or situation they fear in a controlled and safe environment. This allows them to confront their fears and learn that they are not as threatening as they may have initially believed. With the guidance of a trained therapist, individuals can develop coping mechanisms and gradually reduce their anxiety levels.

Another effective treatment option for phobias is medication. While medication alone does not cure phobias, it can help manage the symptoms and reduce anxiety levels. Antianxiety medications, such as benzodiazepines, can provide short-term relief for individuals struggling with severe anxiety. Antidepressants, such as selective serotonin reuptake inhibitors (SSRIs), can also be prescribed to help regulate mood and reduce anxiety in the long term.

In addition to therapy and medication, self-help techniques can also be valuable tools in managing phobias. Deep breathing exercises, meditation, and mindfulness techniques can help individuals relax and reduce anxiety levels. These techniques can be practiced at any time and in any place, making them accessible and bene cial for individuals facing phobias in their daily lives.

Furthermore, support groups can provide individuals with a sense of community and understanding. Connecting with others who have similar experiences can help individuals feel less alone and provide a platform to discuss coping strategies and share successes.

It is important to note that treatment options may vary depending on the severity of the phobia and the individual's speci c needs. It is recommended to consult with a mental health professional to determine the most suitable treatment plan.

In conclusion, treatment options for phobias are diverse and effective. Whether through therapy, medication, self-help techniques, or support groups, individuals can nd ways to overcome their phobias and lead ful lling lives. With the right support and resources, it is possible to conquer even the most debilitating fears and regain control over one's mind.

Chapter 8: Separation Anxiety Disorder

Overview of Separation Anxiety Disorder

Separation Anxiety Disorder (SAD) is a common anxiety disorder that affects individuals across various age groups, including children, adolescents, and adults. It is characterized by excessive fear or worry when separated from individuals or places that provide feelings of security and attachment. This subchapter aims to provide an overview of Separation Anxiety Disorder, exploring its causes, symptoms, and available treatment options.

People with Separation Anxiety Disorder often experience intense distress and anxiety, leading to signi cant impairment in their daily functioning. Children with this disorder may exhibit extreme distress when separated from their primary caregivers, such as parents or close family members. They may refuse to go to school or engage in activities that require separation from their loved ones. Adolescents and adults may also struggle with separation, often avoiding situations that involve leaving home or being alone.

The exact causes of Separation Anxiety Disorder are not fully understood, but several factors are believed to contribute to its development. Genetic predisposition, environmental factors, and brain chemistry abnormalities may all play a role. Additionally, traumatic events, such as the loss of a loved one or a signi cant life change, can trigger or exacerbate symptoms of Separation Anxiety Disorder.

Common symptoms of Separation Anxiety Disorder include excessive distress when anticipating or experiencing separation, persistent worry about the well-being of loved ones, nightmares or trouble sleeping alone, physical complaints (headaches, stomachaches) when separated, and dif culty concentrating or focusing on tasks due to preoccupation with separation-related thoughts.

Fortunately, there are effective treatment options available for individuals with Separation Anxiety Disorder.

Psychotherapy, particularly cognitive-behavioral therapy (CBT), is often recommended. CBT helps individuals identify and challenge negative thoughts and beliefs associated with separation, gradually exposing them to separation situations in a controlled manner. Medication, such as selective serotonin reuptake inhibitors (SSRIs), may also be prescribed in severe cases or when therapy alone is not suf cient.

Understanding Separation Anxiety Disorder is crucial, as it allows individuals and their loved ones to seek appropriate help and support. By recognizing the symptoms and causes, we can work towards managing and overcoming the challenges associated with this disorder. With the right treatment and support, individuals with Separation Anxiety Disorder can lead ful lling lives and develop healthier coping mechanisms to navigate separation-related fears and worries.

Causes and Risk Factors of S aration Anxiety Disorder

Causes and Risk Factors of Separation Anxiety Disorder

Separation anxiety disorder is a type of anxiety disorder characterized by excessive fear or worry when separated from a loved one or familiar environment. Although it is commonly associated with children, it can also affect adults. In this subchapter, we will explore the causes and risk factors that contribute to the development of separation anxiety disorder.

One of the primary causes of separation anxiety disorder is a traumatic experience involving separation or loss. For example, a child who has experienced the sudden death of a parent or caregiver may develop intense anxiety when separated from others. Similarly, adults who have gone through a divorce or the loss of a loved one may also experience separation anxiety.

Genetics and family history can also play a role in the development of separation anxiety disorder. Research suggests that individuals with a family history of anxiety disorders are more likely to develop this particular disorder. This indicates a possible genetic predisposition to anxietyrelated conditions.

Additionally, environmental factors such as parenting style and attachment patterns can contribute to the development of separation anxiety disorder. Children who have been raised in overprotective or overly anxious environments may be more prone to developing this disorder. In contrast, those who have experienced a secure attachment with their caregivers and have been encouraged to explore and develop independence may be less likely to develop separation anxiety disorder.

Certain personality traits and temperament can also increase the risk of developing separation anxiety disorder. Individuals who are naturally more timid, shy, or easily startled may be more vulnerable to developing anxiety-related disorders, including separation anxiety.

Lastly, stressful life events such as moving to a new place, changing schools, or experiencing signi cant life changes can trigger separation anxiety disorder in both children and adults. These events disrupt the familiar routines and environments, leading to heightened anxiety and fear of separation.

Understanding the causes and risk factors of separation anxiety disorder can help us recognize the signs and seek appropriate treatment. It is important to remember that this disorder is treatable, and with the right support and interventions, individuals can learn to manage their anxiety and lead ful lling lives.

Diagnostic Criteria for S aration Anxiety Disorder

Diagnostic Criteria for Separation Anxiety Disorder

Separation Anxiety Disorder is a common anxiety disorder that affects both children and adults. It is characterized by excessive fear or worry about being separated from loved ones or familiar environments. In this subchapter, we will explore the diagnostic criteria for Separation Anxiety Disorder, helping you understand the signs and symptoms to look out for.

To be diagnosed with Separation Anxiety Disorder, an individual must meet speci c criteria outlined in the Diagnostic and Statistical Manual of Mental Disorders (DSM5). These criteria are:

1. Excessive fear or anxiety concerning separation from homeor attachment gures. This fear must be beyond what is appropriate for the individual's developmental level.
2. Persistent worry about losing attachment gures orexperiencing harm when separated from them.
3. Reluctance or refusal to go out or be alone because of fearof separation.
4. Persistent nightmares involving separation-related themes.
5. Physical symptoms, such as headaches, stomachaches, ornausea, when separation is anticipated or occurs.
6. Fear or reluctance to sleep without being near anattachment gure.
7. Repeated nightmares about separation.
8. Excessive distress when separation occurs or is anticipated,lasting at least four weeks in children and six months in adults.

It is important to note that these symptoms must be present for a signi cant amount of time and cause signi cant distress or impairment in various areas of life, such as school, work, or relationships.

Separation Anxiety Disorder can have a signi cant impact on an individual's life, causing disruptions in daily activities and hindering personal growth. However, with proper understanding and support, individuals with this disorder can learn how to manage their anxiety effectively.

If you or someone you know exhibits these symptoms, it is crucial to seek professional help from a mental health provider. They will conduct a comprehensive assessment and develop an appropriate treatment plan, which may include therapy, medication, or a combination of both.

Remember, you are not alone in this journey. Many resources and support groups are available to help individuals with Separation Anxiety Disorder and their loved ones. By understanding the diagnostic criteria, you can take the rst step towards nding the support and guidance needed for a healthier and happier life.

Treatment Options for S)aration Anxiety Disorder

Treatment Options for Separation Anxiety Disorder

Separation anxiety disorder (SAD) is a type of anxiety disorder that affects individuals of all ages, from children to adults. It is characterized by excessive fear or worry when separated from loved ones or familiar surroundings.

Fortunately, there are various treatment options available to help individuals manage and overcome separation anxiety disorder.

One of the most common treatments for separation anxiety disorder is cognitive-behavioral therapy (CBT). CBT aims to change negative thought patterns and behaviors associated with separation anxiety. Through therapy sessions, individuals learn coping mechanisms, relaxation techniques, and strategies to challenge their anxious thoughts. This therapy can be highly effective, providing individuals with the tools they need to manage their anxiety and reduce their symptoms.

In some cases, medication may be prescribed to alleviate the symptoms of separation anxiety disorder. Selective serotonin reuptake inhibitors (SSRIs), such as uoxetine or sertraline, are commonly used to treat anxiety disorders. These medications help regulate the levels of serotonin in the brain, which can help reduce anxiety symptoms. It is important to note that medication should always be prescribed and monitored by a quali ed healthcare professional.

Family therapy can also play a crucial role in the treatment of separation anxiety disorder, especially when it occurs in children. In family therapy, parents and siblings are involved in the treatment process to better understand the disorder and provide support. This therapy can help improve family dynamics, communication, and develop strategies to manage separation anxiety together.

Additionally, lifestyle changes can greatly contribute to the management of separation anxiety disorder. Regular exercise, healthy eating, and suf cient sleep are all important for overall well-being and can help reduce anxiety symptoms. Engaging in activities that promote relaxation and stress reduction, such as yoga or meditation, can also be bene cial.

Support groups and online communities can provide individuals with a sense of belonging and understanding. Connecting with others who are experiencing or have overcome separation anxiety disorder can offer valuable insights, advice, and encouragement. It is important to remember that everyone's experience with separation anxiety disorder is unique, and what works for one person may not work for another.

In conclusion, separation anxiety disorder can be challenging, but with the right treatment options, individuals can effectively manage their symptoms and lead ful lling lives. Cognitive-behavioral therapy, medication, family therapy, lifestyle changes, and support groups are all valuable tools that can aid in the treatment process. Remember, seeking help is a sign of strength, and there is hope for those living with separation anxiety disorder.

Chapter 9: Specific Phobias

Overview of Specific Phobias

Chapter 9: Speci c Phobias

Overview of Speci c Phobias

Speci c phobias are a common type of anxiety disorder that affects millions of people worldwide. These phobias are characterized by an intense and irrational fear of a speci c object, situation, or activity. While it is normal to feel some level of fear or discomfort in certain situations, speci c

phobias create an overwhelming response that can signi cantly impact an individual's daily life.

One of the key features of speci c phobias is the speci city of the fear. Unlike other anxiety disorders that may involve a broader range of triggers, speci c phobias are focused on a particular thing or situation. Some common examples include fear of heights (acrophobia), fear of spiders (arachnophobia), fear of ying (aviophobia), or fear of public speaking (glossophobia).

The origins of speci c phobias can vary. In some cases, they may develop during childhood and persist into adulthood. Others may arise following a traumatic event or a negative experience associated with the phobic stimulus. Additionally, some phobias may be learned from observing others, such as a parent or sibling displaying excessive fear in certain situations.

The impact of speci c phobias on a person's life can be signi cant. Individuals with speci c phobias often go to great lengths to avoid the feared object or situation, which can lead to signi cant limitations in their daily activities. For example, someone with a fear of ying may avoid traveling by air altogether, missing out on important events or opportunities. The avoidance behaviors can also lead to feelings of isolation, frustration, and embarrassment.

Treatment options for speci c phobias are available and can be highly effective. One common approach is cognitivebehavioral therapy (CBT), which involves gradually exposing the individual to the feared object or situation in a controlled and supportive environment. This process, known as exposure therapy, helps the person confront their fears and learn that the anticipated negative outcomes are unlikely to occur.

Medications can also be used to manage the symptoms of speci c phobias, particularly in cases where the fear is severe or signi cantly impacts the person's quality of life. However, medication alone is not considered a long-term solution and is often used in conjunction with therapy.

In conclusion, speci c phobias are a type of anxiety disorder characterized by an intense and irrational fear of a speci c object, situation, or activity. These phobias can signi cantly impact an individual's daily life, leading to avoidance behaviors and feelings of isolation. However, effective treatment options, such as cognitive-behavioral therapy and medication, are available to help individuals overcome their speci c phobias and regain control of their lives.

Causes and Risk Factors of Specific Phobias

Causes and Risk Factors of Specic Phobias

Understanding the causes and risk factors associated with speci c phobias is crucial in order to comprehend the complex nature of anxiety disorders. Speci c phobias are characterized by an intense and irrational fear of a speci c object, situation, or activity. While these fears may seem irrational to others, they can be overwhelming and debilitating for those who experience them. In this subchapter, we will explore the various factors that contribute to the development of speci c phobias.

One of the primary causes of speci c phobias is a traumatic or distressing experience related to the feared object or situation. For example, someone who has experienced a dog bite may develop a phobia of dogs. Traumatic events can create a lasting impression on the mind, leading to an association between the fear-inducing stimulus and the negative experience. This association can trigger extreme fear and anxiety when confronted with the phobic stimulus in the future.

Another important factor in the development of speci c

phobias is learned behavior. Children often learn fear from observing their parents or other signi cant gures in their lives. If a parent has a phobia, their child may adopt the same fear, even without having a direct traumatic experience. This learned behavior can also occur through media exposure, where individuals may develop fears of certain animals or situations after watching alarming or distressing portrayals.

Genetics and hereditary factors also play a role in the development of specific phobias. Research suggests that individuals with a family history of anxiety disorders and phobias are more likely to develop specific phobias themselves. This suggests a genetic predisposition to these disorders, although the specific genes involved have yet to be fully identified.

Personality traits and temperament can also contribute to the risk of developing specific phobias. Individuals who are naturally more anxious, timid, or sensitive may be more prone to developing phobias. Additionally, individuals with a tendency to catastrophize or overestimate the likelihood of negative outcomes are more likely to develop specific phobias.

It is important to note that while these factors contribute to the development of specific phobias, they do not guarantee the development of a phobia. Each individual's experience is unique, and a combination of these factors may interact differently in each case.

In conclusion, understanding the causes and risk factors of specific phobias provides valuable insight into the complex nature of anxiety disorders. Traumatic experiences, learned behavior, genetics, and personality traits all contribute to the development of specific phobias. By recognizing these factors, individuals can gain a better understanding of their own fears and seek appropriate support and treatment.

Diagnostic Criteria for Specific Phobias

Speci c phobias are a common type of anxiety disorder that affect millions of people worldwide. These phobias are characterized by an intense and irrational fear of a speci c object, situation, or activity. While it is normal to experience some level of fear or discomfort in certain situations, speci c phobias go beyond this and can signi cantly impact a person's daily life.

To diagnose a speci c phobia, mental health professionals rely on speci c criteria outlined in the Diagnostic and Statistical Manual of Mental Disorders (DSM-5). These criteria help determine if a person's fear quali es as a phobia and if it requires treatment. Here are the diagnostic criteria for speci c phobias:

1. Marked fear or anxiety: The person experiences an intenseand persistent fear or anxiety when confronted with the phobic stimulus. This fear is excessive and unreasonable, considering the actual danger posed by the object or situation.
2. Immediate anxiety response: The fear or anxiety istriggered immediately upon exposure to the phobic stimulus, or even by just thinking about it.
3. Avoidance behavior: The person actively avoids the phobicstimulus or endures it with intense distress. They might go to great lengths to avoid situations or places that could trigger their fear.
4. Interference with daily life: The fear, anxiety, or

avoidancesigni cantly disrupts the person's daily routine, social activities, relationships, or occupational functioning.
5. Duration: The symptoms have persisted for at least sixmonths, causing distress and impairment.

It is important to note that not all fears are considered speci c phobias. Some common speci c phobias include fear of heights (acrophobia), fear of spiders (arachnophobia), fear of ying (aviophobia), and fear of public speaking (glossophobia). However, speci c phobias can encompass a wide range of objects or situations.

If you suspect you may have a speci c phobia, it is essential to seek help from a mental health professional. They will conduct a thorough assessment to determine the speci c phobia and develop an appropriate treatment plan. Treatment options for speci c phobias can include cognitive-behavioral therapy (CBT), exposure therapy, and medication, depending on the severity and impact of the phobia on the individual's life.

Understanding the diagnostic criteria for speci c phobias can help individuals recognize their fears and seek appropriate treatment. Remember, you are not alone, and help is available to overcome your speci c phobia and regain control over your life.

Treatment Options for Specific Phobias

Treatment Options for Specic Phobias

Speci c phobias are one of the most common anxiety disorders, affecting millions of people worldwide. These phobias are characterized by intense and irrational fears of speci c objects, situations, or activities. While the fear may seem irrational to others, it can cause signi cant distress and interfere with daily life for those experiencing it.

Fortunately, there are effective treatment options available to help individuals overcome speci c phobias and regain control over their lives. In this subchapter, we will explore some of the most successful approaches used to treat these anxiety disorders.

1. Cognitive-behavioral therapy (CBT): CBT is a widelyrecognized and effective form of therapy for speci c phobias. This type of therapy helps individuals identify and challenge negative thought patterns and beliefs associated with their phobia. Through gradual exposure to the feared object or situation, individuals learn to reframe their thoughts and develop healthier coping mechanisms.

2. Exposure therapy: Exposure therapy is a key component ofCBT and involves gradually exposing individuals to their phobia in a controlled and safe environment. This exposure helps reduce the fear response and desensitize the individual to the phobic stimulus. Over time, repeated exposure can lead to a

decrease in anxiety and an increased ability to manage and confront the phobia.

3. Medications: In some cases, medication may be prescribedto help manage the symptoms of speci c phobias.

Antidepressants and anti-anxiety medications can help reduce anxiety and provide temporary relief. However, it's important to note that medication alone is not a long-term solution and should be used in conjunction with therapy for optimal results.

1. Mindfulness and relaxation techniques: Learning relaxationtechniques, such as deep breathing exercises and meditation, can help individuals manage their anxiety and reduce the physical symptoms associated with speci c phobias. By practicing mindfulness, individuals can develop a greater sense of control and learn to stay present in the moment, rather than focusing on their fears.

2. Support groups: Joining a support group can provideindividuals with a sense of community and understanding. Sharing experiences and coping strategies with others who have similar phobias can be empowering and reassuring. Support groups also offer a safe space to discuss fears and challenges openly, without judgment.

Remember, seeking professional help is essential when dealing with speci c phobias. A quali ed therapist or mental health professional can tailor treatment to individual needs and guide individuals through the process of overcoming their fears. With the right treatment approach and support, it is possible to conquer speci c phobias and live a life free from the constraints of anxiety.

Chapter 10: Other Anxiety Disorders

Overview of Other Anxiety Disorders (Selective

Mutism, Agoraphobia, etc.)

In addition to the well-known anxiety disorders like generalized anxiety disorder, panic disorder, and social anxiety disorder, there are several other anxiety disorders that are less commonly talked about but equally important to understand. This subchapter aims to shed light on some of these lesser-known anxiety disorders, including selective mutism and agoraphobia, among others.

Selective mutism is an anxiety disorder primarily seen in children, where they consistently fail to speak in certain situations, despite being perfectly capable of speech in other settings. Children with selective mutism often experience extreme anxiety and fear when confronted with unfamiliar people or situations, leading to their inability to speak. This disorder can signi cantly impact a child's social and academic development, making early identi cation and intervention crucial.

Agoraphobia is another anxiety disorder that is often misunderstood or overlooked. It is characterized by an intense fear of being in situations where escape might be dif cult or embarrassing, leading to avoidance of places such as crowded areas, public transportation, or open spaces. People with agoraphobia may become housebound or restrict their activities, causing signi cant distress and disruption to their daily lives.

Other anxiety disorders covered in this subchapter include speci c phobias, such as fear of heights, spiders, or ying, which can cause overwhelming anxiety and avoidance behaviors. Additionally, the chapter explores separation anxiety disorder, which is commonly seen in children and involves excessive fear or anxiety when separated from attachment gures, leading to distress and impairment in their daily functioning.

Understanding these various anxiety disorders is crucial for the general public as they can affect individuals of all ages, genders, and backgrounds. By familiarizing ourselves with the A-Z of anxiety disorders, we can develop empathy and support those who may be struggling with these conditions.

This subchapter aims to provide a comprehensive overview of these lesser-known anxiety disorders, offering insights into their symptoms, causes, and available treatments. By promoting awareness and understanding, we hope to reduce stigma and encourage individuals to seek help when needed.

If you or someone you know is experiencing symptoms of any anxiety disorder, it is essential to consult with a mental health professional who can provide a proper diagnosis and develop an appropriate treatment plan. Remember, anxiety disorders are treatable, and with the right support, individuals can lead ful lling and anxiety-free lives.

Causes and Risk Factors of Other Anxiety Disorders

Anxiety disorders encompass a wide range of conditions that can signi cantly impact an individual's daily life. While each disorder has its unique set of causes and risk factors, there are some commonalities that can help us better understand their origins. In this subchapter, we will explore the causes and risk factors of other anxiety disorders, shedding light on the factors that contribute to these conditions.

One of the primary causes of anxiety disorders is believed to be a combination of genetic and environmental factors. Research suggests that certain individuals may be genetically predisposed to developing anxiety disorders, meaning they have a higher likelihood of experiencing anxiety-related symptoms. However, it is important to note that having a genetic predisposition does not guarantee the development of an anxiety disorder. Environmental factors, such as childhood trauma, chronic stress, or major life changes, can trigger the onset of anxiety disorders in individuals with a genetic vulnerability.

Another signi cant risk factor for anxiety disorders is a history of other mental health conditions. Individuals who have previously experienced depression, post-traumatic stress disorder (PTSD), or obsessive-compulsive disorder (OCD) are more likely to develop an anxiety disorder. This suggests a common underlying vulnerability or shared biological mechanisms between these conditions.

Furthermore, certain personality traits can increase the risk of developing anxiety disorders. People who are naturally more anxious, perfectionistic, or have a low tolerance for uncertainty may be prone to experiencing excessive worry and fear, leading to the development of an anxiety disorder. Additionally, individuals who have a history of substance abuse or addiction are at a higher risk of developing anxiety disorders as these substances can worsen anxiety symptoms.

Interestingly, there is evidence to suggest that cultural and societal factors play a role in the development of anxiety disorders. Different cultures may have varying levels of stigma surrounding mental health, access to healthcare, and social support systems, which can impact an individual's risk of developing an anxiety disorder. For instance, individuals from cultures that value stoicism and discourage emotional expression may be more likely to internalize their anxiety, potentially exacerbating their symptoms.

Diagnostic Criteria for Other Anxiety Disorders

Understanding the causes and risk factors of anxiety disorders is crucial for early identi cation, prevention, and effective treatment. By recognizing the various factors that contribute to these disorders, we can work towards reducing stigma, improving access to mental health resources, and promoting overall well-being for individuals experiencing anxiety.

Diagnostic Criteria for Other Anxiety Disorders

In addition to well-known anxiety disorders such as generalized anxiety disorder (GAD), panic disorder, and social anxiety disorder, there are several other anxiety disorders that are less commonly discussed but still signi cant. This subchapter aims to shed light on these lesser-known anxiety disorders, providing a better understanding of their diagnostic criteria.

1. Speci c Phobias:

Speci c phobias are intense and irrational fears of speci c objects or situations. The fear is excessive and leads to avoidance behaviors that can signi cantly impact a person's daily life. Diagnostic criteria include a persistent fear triggered by a speci c object or situation, immediate anxiety response when exposed to the fear trigger, and recognition that the fear is excessive.

1. Separation Anxiety Disorder:

Often associated with children, separation anxiety disorder can also affect adults. It involves excessive anxiety when separated from a person or place that provides security. Symptoms include distress when anticipating or experiencing separation, persistent worry about harm befalling loved ones, and reluctance to be alone.

1. Selective Mutism:

Selective mutism is characterized by an inability to speak in speci c social situations, despite being able to speak comfortably in other settings. Diagnostic criteria include consistent failure to speak in speci c situations, lasting for at least one month, and interference with educational or occupational achievements.

1. Substance/Medication-Induced Anxiety Disorder:

Anxiety symptoms can be triggered or worsened by substance abuse or withdrawal, certain medications, or exposure to toxins. Diagnostic criteria include prominent anxiety symptoms that are a direct result of substance use, medication, or toxin exposure, and evidence from history, physical examination, or laboratory ndings.

1. Other Speci ed Anxiety Disorder and Unspeci ed

AnxietyDisorder:

These categories are used when an individual's symptoms do not meet the speci c criteria for any other anxiety disorder but still cause signi cant distress and impairment. The symptoms may not t precisely into any de ned disorder, but they are nonetheless distressing and require attention.

Understanding the diagnostic criteria for these other anxiety disorders can help individuals and their loved ones recognize when they may be experiencing more than just "ordinary" anxiety. If any of these disorders resonate with you or someone you know, it is essential to seek professional help for a proper diagnosis and appropriate treatment.

Remember, anxiety disorders are common and treatable. With the right support and guidance, individuals can learn to manage their anxiety and lead ful lling lives.

Treatment Options for Other Anxiety Disorders

In this subchapter, we will explore the various treatment options available for anxiety disorders that fall under the category of "Other Anxiety Disorders." While anxiety disorders can be challenging to cope with, it is important to remember that effective treatment options are available to help individuals regain control of their lives and nd relief from their symptoms.

One of the most common treatment approaches for anxiety disorders is psychotherapy, also known as talk therapy. Different types of therapy, such as cognitive-behavioral therapy (CBT) and exposure therapy, have proven to be highly effective in treating anxiety disorders. CBT focuses on identifying and changing negative thought patterns and behaviors that contribute to anxiety, while exposure therapy gradually exposes individuals to their fears in a safe and controlled environment, helping them to overcome their anxieties.

Medication can also be a valuable tool in the treatment of anxiety disorders. Antidepressant medications, such as selective serotonin reuptake inhibitors (SSRIs), are often prescribed to help regulate brain chemistry and reduce anxiety symptoms. It is important to note that medication should always be prescribed and monitored by a quali ed healthcare professional.

In addition to therapy and medication, self-help strategies can be bene cial in managing anxiety disorders. These strategies may include relaxation techniques, such as deep breathing exercises and mindfulness meditation, which help individuals to calm their minds and bodies. Regular exercise, a healthy diet, and getting enough sleep can also contribute to overall well-being and reduce anxiety symptoms.

Furthermore, support from friends, family, and support groups can play a crucial role in the recovery process. Sharing experiences with others who have similar struggles can provide a sense of validation and encouragement. It is important for individuals with anxiety disorders to reach out for support and not isolate themselves.

In conclusion, anxiety disorders can be effectively managed with a combination of psychotherapy, medication, self-help strategies, and support from loved ones. It is essential for individuals to seek professional help and explore the various treatment options available to nd what works best for them. Remember, you are not alone in your journey, and there is hope for a life free from the grips of anxiety.

Chapter 11: Coping Strategies for Anxiety Disorders

Lifestyle Changes to Manage Anxiety Disorders

Living with anxiety disorders can be overwhelming and challenging, but it is possible to regain control and nd peace within yourself. In addition to seeking professional help and treatment, making certain lifestyle changes can signi cantly improve your overall well-being and manage anxiety disorders effectively. This chapter focuses on exploring various lifestyle changes that can help individuals cope with anxiety disorders and enhance their quality of life.

Physical activity is a crucial aspect of managing anxiety disorders. Engaging in regular exercise such as walking, jogging, or yoga can help release endorphins, the body's natural mood-lifters, and reduce anxiety symptoms. Exercise also promotes better sleep and increases overall energy levels, resulting in a more positive mindset.

Maintaining a healthy diet is equally important. Avoiding excessive caffeine, alcohol, and processed foods can help stabilize your mood and reduce anxiety-related symptoms.

Incorporating foods rich in omega-3 fatty acids, such as fatty sh, walnuts, and axseeds, can also help alleviate anxiety symptoms.

Implementing relaxation techniques into your daily routine can signi cantly reduce anxiety. Practices such as deep breathing exercises, meditation, and mindfulness can help calm the mind and promote relaxation. These techniques can be integrated into your daily life, whether it's taking a few minutes to focus on your breath or practicing mindfulness during routine activities like eating or showering.

Establishing a consistent sleep routine is vital for managing anxiety disorders. Lack of sleep can exacerbate anxiety symptoms, making it crucial to prioritize quality rest. Creating a relaxing bedtime routine, limiting exposure to electronic devices before bed, and ensuring a comfortable sleep environment can aid in achieving a restful night's sleep.

Social support plays a signi cant role in managing anxiety disorders. Reach out to family, friends, or support groups who can provide understanding, guidance, and encouragement. Sharing your experiences with others who have similar conditions can help reduce feelings of isolation and provide valuable insights into coping mechanisms.

Finally, it is essential to manage stress effectively in order to control anxiety disorders. Incorporating stress-reducing activities such as reading, listening to music, practicing hobbies, or engaging in creative outlets can help divert your mind from anxious thoughts and promote relaxation.

By implementing these lifestyle changes, individuals can take proactive steps toward managing their anxiety disorders and improving their overall well-being. Remember that everyone's journey is unique, so be patient with yourself and celebrate small victories along the way. With determination and the right support, it is possible to nd inner peace and live a ful lling life despite anxiety disorders.

Note: This content is a general guide and should not replace professional advice. Please consult a healthcare professional for personalized recommendations and treatment options.

Therapy and Counseling Options## Therapy and Counseling Options

When it comes to managing anxiety disorders, therapy and counseling play a crucial role in helping individuals navigate their way to a healthier mental state. While medications can be effective in some cases, therapy offers a holistic approach that addresses the root causes of anxiety disorders and equips individuals with coping mechanisms to better manage their symptoms.

One of the most widely recognized forms of therapy for anxiety disorders is cognitive-behavioral therapy (CBT). This type of therapy focuses on identifying and challenging negative thought patterns and behaviors that contribute to anxiety. By helping individuals reframe their thoughts and develop healthier coping strategies, CBT empowers them to take control of their anxiety. CBT is often combined with exposure therapy, where individuals gradually face their fears in a safe and controlled environment, desensitizing themselves to anxiety triggers.

Another effective therapy option is psychodynamic therapy, which delves into the unconscious mind to explore the underlying causes of anxiety disorders. By examining past experiences and relationships, individuals can gain insight into the root causes of their anxiety and work towards resolving unresolved con icts. This therapy option is particularly bene cial for individuals who have experienced trauma or have deeply rooted issues contributing to their anxiety.

For those seeking a more hands-on approach, alternative therapy options such as art therapy, music therapy, and animal-assisted therapy can provide unique outlets for selfexpression and relaxation. Art therapy allows individuals to explore their emotions through various art forms, while music therapy uses music as a therapeutic tool to improve mood and reduce anxiety. Animal-assisted therapy involves interacting with animals, which has been shown to reduce stress and promote a sense of calm.

In addition to therapy, counseling can be a valuable resource for individuals with anxiety disorders. Counseling provides a supportive and non-judgmental environment for individuals to express their fears and concerns. Counselors can offer guidance, advice, and practical strategies to help individuals cope with their anxiety on a day-to-day basis. They can also assist individuals in developing healthy lifestyle habits, such as exercise, proper nutrition, and stress management techniques, which can signi cantly reduce anxiety symptoms.

It is important to note that therapy and counseling options can be tailored to suit individual needs and preferences. What works for one person may not work for another, so it may take some trial and error to nd the right approach. The key is to seek professional help and be open to exploring different options until the right t is found.

Overall, therapy and counseling are essential components in the treatment of anxiety disorders. They provide individuals with the tools and support they need to combat their anxiety and regain control of their lives. By addressing the underlying causes of anxiety and equipping individuals with effective coping strategies, therapy and counseling can pave the way towards a brighter and anxiety-free future.

Medications for Anxiety Disorders

Medications for Anxiety Disorders

Anxiety disorders are a common mental health condition affecting millions of people worldwide. While there are various treatment options available, including therapy and lifestyle changes, medications can also play a crucial role in managing these disorders. In this subchapter, we will explore the different types of medications commonly prescribed for anxiety disorders.

One of the most commonly prescribed medications for anxiety disorders is selective serotonin reuptake inhibitors (SSRIs). SSRIs work by increasing the levels of serotonin, a neurotransmitter that regulates mood, in the brain. These medications are considered effective in treating various anxiety disorders, including generalized anxiety disorder (GAD), social anxiety disorder, and panic disorder. Some commonly prescribed SSRIs include Prozac, Zoloft, and Lexapro.

Another class of medications used for anxiety disorders is benzodiazepines. Benzodiazepines work by enhancing the effects of gamma-aminobutyric acid (GABA), a neurotransmitter that helps calm the brain. These medications provide rapid relief from anxiety symptoms and are often prescribed for short-term use or during acute episodes. However, they can be habit-forming and may cause drowsiness and cognitive impairment. Therefore, they are generally used cautiously and for a limited duration.

In addition to SSRIs and benzodiazepines, other medications, such as buspirone and beta-blockers, may be prescribed for speci c anxiety disorders. Buspirone is a non-addictive medication that acts on serotonin receptors, helping to reduce anxiety symptoms. Beta-blockers, often used for heart conditions, can also be helpful in managing the physical symptoms of anxiety, such as rapid heartbeat and trembling.

It is important to note that medication alone is not a cure for anxiety disorders. These medications are typically used in conjunction with therapy and lifestyle modi cations to achieve the best outcomes. Each individual's response to medication may vary, and it may take some time to nd the right medication and dosage that works best for them. Regular communication with a healthcare professional is essential to monitor the effectiveness of the medication and any potential side effects.

While medications can offer signi cant relief for those with anxiety disorders, they are not suitable for everyone. It is crucial to consult with a healthcare provider who specializes in mental health to determine the most appropriate treatment plan for an individual's speci c anxiety disorder. With the right combination of medication, therapy, and support, individuals can effectively manage their anxiety and lead ful lling lives.

Self-Help Techniques## Self-Help Techniques

When it comes to managing anxiety disorders, self-help techniques can be an invaluable tool in your journey towards mental well-being. These techniques empower individuals to take control of their thoughts, emotions, and behaviors, offering practical strategies to cope with anxiety and reduce its impact on daily life. In this chapter, we will explore a variety of self-help techniques that can be applied to various anxiety disorders, offering a comprehensive A-Z guide to managing anxiety.

One of the most effective self-help techniques is practicing relaxation exercises. Deep breathing, progressive muscle relaxation, and meditation can all help calm the mind and body, reducing feelings of anxiety. By incorporating these techniques into your daily routine, you can cultivate a sense of inner peace and tranquility.

Another useful technique is cognitive restructuring, which involves identifying and challenging negative thought patterns. Anxiety often stems from distorted thinking, such as catastrophizing or overgeneralizing. By learning to question these thoughts and replace them with more realistic and positive ones, you can alleviate anxiety and promote a more balanced mindset.

Additionally, engaging in regular physical exercise has been proven to reduce anxiety levels. Exercise releases endorphins, which are natural mood boosters, and can help distract the mind from anxious thoughts. Whether it's going for a walk, practicing yoga, or participating in a team sport, nding an activity that you enjoy and can commit to can have a signi cant impact on your overall well-being.

Furthermore, maintaining a healthy lifestyle through proper nutrition and sleep is paramount in managing anxiety. Certain foods, such as those rich in omega-3 fatty acids, have been shown to have calming effects on the brain. Additionally, ensuring you get adequate sleep can help regulate mood and reduce anxiety symptoms.

Lastly, seeking support from others who are experiencing similar challenges can be incredibly bene cial. Support groups, therapy, and online communities provide a safe space to share experiences, gain insights, and learn from others. Connecting with others who understand your struggles can help reduce feelings of isolation and provide encouragement in your journey towards recovery.

In conclusion, self-help techniques are powerful tools that can help individuals navigate the complexities of anxiety disorders. By incorporating relaxation exercises, cognitive restructuring, exercise, healthy lifestyle choices, and seeking support, you can actively manage your anxiety and improve your overall well-being. Remember, everyone's journey is unique, so explore these techniques and nd what works best for you. With dedication and perseverance, you can regain control of your mind and live a ful lling life free from the constraints of anxiety.

Chapter 12: Overcoming Stigma and Seeking Help

Recognizing the Stigma Associated with Anxiety Disorders

Anxiety disorders affect millions of people worldwide, yet they are often misunderstood and stigmatized by society. This subchapter aims to shed light on the misconceptions surrounding anxiety disorders and highlight the importance of recognizing and addressing the stigma associated with them.

Firstly, it is crucial to understand that anxiety disorders are real medical conditions. They are not simply a result of personal weakness or a lack of willpower. Anxiety disorders can signi cantly impact a person's daily life, causing excessive worrying, panic attacks, and other distressing symptoms. It is essential for the general public to recognize that individuals with anxiety disorders are not choosing to feel anxious; rather, their condition is a result of complex interactions between genetic, environmental, and neurological factors.

Unfortunately, the stigma surrounding anxiety disorders can prevent individuals from seeking help and support. Many people with anxiety disorders fear being judged or seen as weak if they disclose their condition. This stigma can lead to feelings of shame and isolation, worsening the symptoms and hindering recovery. It is crucial for society to create an environment that encourages open discussions about mental health and supports those who are struggling.

Furthermore, recognizing the diversity within the A - Z of anxiety disorders can help combat the stigma. Anxiety disorders encompass a broad range of conditions, including generalized anxiety disorder, social anxiety disorder, obsessive-compulsive disorder, and post-traumatic stress disorder, among others. Each disorder presents unique challenges and requires tailored treatments. By understanding the different manifestations of anxiety disorders, the general public can foster empathy and provide appropriate support to those affected.

Education and awareness play a vital role in dismantling the stigma associated with anxiety disorders. By educating ourselves about the causes, symptoms, and treatments of these disorders, we can challenge misconceptions and promote a more compassionate society. It is important to emphasize that seeking help for an anxiety disorder is a sign of strength, not weakness. Encouraging open conversations, supporting mental health initiatives, and advocating for equal access to mental health services are all ways in which we can combat the stigma surrounding anxiety disorders.

In conclusion, recognizing the stigma associated with anxiety disorders is essential for creating a society that supports and understands individuals affected by these conditions. By dispelling misconceptions, promoting empathy, and encouraging open conversations, we can foster a more inclusive environment for those living with anxiety disorders. Together, we can break down the barriers of stigma and ensure that individuals with anxiety disorders receive the understanding and support they deserve.

Importance of Seeking Professional Help

Importance of Seeking Professional Help

Subchapter: Importance of Seeking Professional Help
Introduction:

When it comes to anxiety disorders, seeking professional help is of utmost importance. While some individuals may be hesitant to reach out for assistance, understanding the signi cance of professional guidance can greatly improve the management and treatment of anxiety disorders. In this subchapter, we will explore the various reasons why seeking professional help is crucial for individuals experiencing anxiety disorders.

1. Accurate Diagnosis:

Anxiety disorders encompass a wide range of conditions, each with its own unique symptoms and treatment options. Consulting a professional, such as a psychologist or psychiatrist, ensures an accurate diagnosis. These experts possess the knowledge and experience to differentiate between different disorders, helping individuals receive appropriate treatment tailored to their speci c needs.

1. Personalized Treatment:

Professional help provides access to personalized treatment plans. Anxiety disorders are not one-size- ts-all, and what works for one person may not work for another. By consulting with a professional, individuals can receive tailored interventions, including therapy, medication, or a combination of both. These customized treatment plans increase the chances of successful management and recovery.

1. Expert Guidance:

Anxiety disorders can be overwhelming, leaving individuals feeling helpless and lost. Seeking professional help allows individuals to bene t from expert guidance and support. Professionals can educate individuals about their speci c anxiety disorder, helping them understand its underlying causes and triggers. They can also teach coping mechanisms, relaxation techniques, and provide valuable insight into managing anxiety-related symptoms effectively.

1. Monitoring Progress:

Regular appointments with a professional enable individuals to monitor their progress effectively. Anxiety disorders can be chronic conditions, and it is essential to track improvement over time. Professionals can assess the effectiveness of the chosen treatment plan, make adjustments if necessary, and provide ongoing support throughout the recovery process.

1. Addressing Co-occurring Disorders:

Many individuals with anxiety disorders also experience cooccurring mental health conditions, such as depression or substance abuse. Seeking professional help ensures that all underlying issues are properly addressed. Professionals can identify and treat co-occurring disorders, preventing them from exacerbating the symptoms of anxiety disorders.

Conclusion:

Seeking professional help is a vital step in managing anxiety disorders effectively. With accurate diagnosis, personalized treatment plans, expert guidance, progress monitoring, and the addressing of co-occurring disorders, professionals play a crucial role in helping individuals regain control over their lives. If you or someone you know is struggling with an anxiety disorder, don't hesitate to reach out to a quali ed professional who can provide the support and guidance needed to navigate the path towards recovery.

Encouraging Support and Understanding from Loved Ones

Encouraging Support and Understanding from Loved Ones

Living with anxiety disorders can be a challenging experience, not just for the individuals dealing with them, but also for their loved ones. Often, those who have never experienced anxiety rsthand may nd it dif cult to comprehend the full extent of what their loved ones are going through. In order to foster a supportive and understanding environment, it is essential for loved ones to educate themselves about the A-Z of anxiety disorders.

First and foremost, it is crucial to realize that anxiety disorders are real and can signi cantly impact a person's daily life. They are not simply a result of overthinking or a lack of willpower. By understanding this, loved ones can avoid unintentionally diminishing the severity of their loved one's struggles.

One effective way to encourage support is by cultivating open and honest communication. Create a safe space for your loved one to express their feelings, fears, and concerns without judgment. Listening attentively and validating their experiences can help alleviate their anxiety. Remember, anxiety disorders are not logical, so it is essential to approach conversations with empathy and understanding.

Educate yourself about the speci c anxiety disorder your loved one is experiencing. Different anxiety disorders manifest in diverse ways, so familiarize yourself with the symptoms, triggers, and potential coping mechanisms associated with their particular condition. This knowledge will enable you to provide appropriate support and assistance when needed.

Encouraging your loved one to seek professional help is also crucial. Therapy and medication can play a signi cant role in managing anxiety disorders. Offer to accompany them to appointments or assist with researching reputable therapists in your area. By taking an active role in their treatment process, you demonstrate your support and dedication to their well-being.

Additionally, consider educating other family members and friends about anxiety disorders. By spreading awareness and dispelling misconceptions, you can foster a more supportive network for your loved one. Encourage others to be patient, compassionate, and understanding, and emphasize that anxiety disorders are not something that can be easily controlled or "snapped out of."

In conclusion, supporting a loved one with an anxiety disorder requires empathy, understanding, and education. By actively educating yourself, cultivating open communication, and encouraging professional help, you can create an environment that fosters support and understanding. Remember, your loved one's journey with anxiety disorders is unique, and your role as a supportive gure can make a signi cant difference in their overall well-being.

Chapter 13: Living with Anxiety

Disorders

Nurturing Relationships while Managing Anxiety Disorders

Anxiety disorders can be overwhelming, causing distress and interfering with daily life. But managing these disorders doesn't mean you have to isolate yourself from the world or let your relationships suffer. In fact, nurturing relationships can play a crucial role in managing anxiety disorders effectively. This subchapter aims to explore how to maintain healthy relationships while dealing with anxiety, offering tips and insights for individuals with any type of anxiety disorder.

1. Communication is key: Open and honest communicationwith your loved ones is vital. Explain your anxiety disorder to them, helping them understand what you're going through. Share your fears and concerns, allowing them to offer support and empathy. This will foster a more understanding and supportive environment.

2. Educate your inner circle: Provide your close friends andfamily with resources about anxiety disorders. Encourage them to learn more about the speci c type

of anxiety disorder you have. This knowledge will empower them to be more compassionate and accommodating when anxiety strikes.

3. Set boundaries: Recognize your limits and communicatethem to your loved ones. Let them know when you need some time alone or when certain situations may trigger your anxiety. Setting boundaries ensures that your relationships are built on respect and understanding.

4. Seek professional help together: If you're comfortable,invite your partner or close family member to attend therapy sessions with you. This can help them gain insights into your condition and provide them with tools to support you effectively.

Inside the Mind: Exploring A - Z of Anxiety Disorders

5. Encourage open conversations about mental health: Break the stigma surrounding mental health by initiating conversations about anxiety disorders. By normalizing these discussions, you create a safe space for your loved ones to share their concerns and learn more about mental health.

6. Practice self-care: Prioritize self-care to manage your anxiety effectively. Engage in activities that bring you joy and relaxation, and make sure to communicate your needs to your loved ones. By taking care of yourself, you'll be better equipped to nurture your relationships.

Remember, nurturing relationships is a two-way street. While it's crucial to communicate your needs and struggles, it's equally important to listen and support your loved ones in return. Building a strong support system is essential in managing anxiety disorders effectively. With open communication, empathy, and understanding, you can create a network of relationships that provide comfort and positivity on your journey towards mental well-being.

Impact of Anxiety Disorders on Work and Education

Subchapter: Impact of Anxiety Disorders on Work and

Education

Anxiety disorders can have a profound impact on various aspects of our lives, including our ability to perform well in work and education. This subchapter aims to shed light on the speci c challenges individuals with anxiety disorders may face in these domains and provide some practical tips for managing anxiety in these settings.

In the workplace, anxiety disorders can manifest in a number of ways. Generalized Anxiety Disorder (GAD) may result in excessive worry about work tasks, leading to dif culty concentrating and making decisions. Social Anxiety Disorder can make it challenging to interact with colleagues or participate in meetings, potentially hindering career growth. Panic Disorder may cause sudden panic attacks that can be disruptive to daily work routines.

For those pursuing education, anxiety disorders can pose unique obstacles. Students with Separation Anxiety Disorder may struggle with leaving home for school, leading to absenteeism. Test anxiety can signi cantly impact academic performance and cause extreme stress before exams. Speci c Phobias, such as the fear of public speaking, can make class presentations a daunting experience.

The impact of anxiety disorders on work and education extends beyond the individual. Employers and educational institutions also need to be aware of the challenges faced by individuals with anxiety disorders. Creating a supportive environment that fosters open communication and understanding can go a long way in helping these individuals thrive.

To manage anxiety disorders in work and education settings, there are several strategies that can be helpful. Seeking professional help, such as therapy or counseling, can provide individuals with the tools to manage their anxiety effectively. Learning relaxation techniques, like deep breathing or mindfulness, can help reduce anxiety symptoms in highpressure situations. Developing healthy coping mechanisms, such as exercise or hobbies, can also aid in managing anxiety on a daily basis.

Furthermore, employers and educational institutions can implement accommodations to support individuals with anxiety disorders. Flexible work or study arrangements, such as remote work or extended deadlines, can help alleviate stress. Providing access to mental health resources and offering employee assistance programs can also make a signi cant difference.

Inside the Mind: Exploring A - Z of Anxiety Disorders

Inside the Mind: Exploring Anxiety Disorders

In conclusion, anxiety disorders can have a signi cant impact on work and education. By raising awareness, promoting understanding, and implementing appropriate support systems, we can create environments that enable individuals with anxiety disorders to reach their full potential in both their professional and educational endeavors.

Strategies for Self-Care and Stress Management

In today's fast-paced and demanding world, it is crucial to prioritize self-care and stress management, especially for individuals dealing with anxiety disorders. Taking care of our mental and emotional well-being is essential for leading a ful lling and healthy life. This subchapter will provide you with practical strategies to incorporate into your daily routine to effectively manage stress and anxiety.

1. Practice Mindfulness: Mindfulness is the practice of beingfully present in the moment, without judgment. By focusing on the present and letting go of worries about the past or future, you can reduce anxiety. Simple activities like deep breathing exercises, meditation, or taking a walk in nature can help you cultivate mindfulness.

2. Prioritize Self-Care: Make self-care a non-negotiable partof your routine. Engage in activities that bring you joy and relaxation, such as reading, taking baths, practicing yoga, or spending time with loved ones. Taking care of your physical health, such as getting enough sleep, eating nutritious meals, and exercising regularly, is also vital for managing stress.

3. Establish Boundaries: Learn to say no and set boundaries toprotect your mental and emotional well-being. It's okay to prioritize your needs and limit excessive commitments that may overwhelm you. Communicate your limitations to others, and don't hesitate to ask for support when needed.

4. Seek Support: You don't have to face anxiety disordersalone. Reach out to trusted friends, family members, or support groups who can offer understanding and encouragement. Consider seeking professional help from therapists or counselors who specialize in anxiety disorders. They can provide valuable guidance and teach you coping mechanisms tailored to your speci c needs.

5. Engage in Relaxation Techniques: Experiment with

variousrelaxation techniques to nd what works best for you. Deep breathing exercises, progressive muscle relaxation, guided imagery, or listening to calming music can help you relax and reduce anxiety.

6. Challenge Negative Thoughts: Anxiety disorders ofteninvolve distorted thinking patterns. Learn to identify and challenge negative thoughts that contribute to your anxiety.

Replace them with more realistic and positive thoughts. Cognitive-behavioral therapy (CBT) techniques can be particularly helpful in this process.

Remember, managing anxiety disorders is a journey, and what works for one person may not work for another. Be patient with yourself and don't be afraid to try different strategies until you nd what resonates with you. By prioritizing self-care and stress management, you can take control of your anxiety and lead a more ful lling life.

Chapter 14: Research and Future Directions

Current Research on Anxiety Disorders

In recent years, there has been signi cant progress in the eld of anxiety disorders research, shedding light on the causes, symptoms, and treatment options for various types of anxiety disorders. This chapter aims to provide an overview of the latest research ndings in the A-Z of anxiety disorders, offering hope and understanding to those who may be struggling with these conditions.

Researchers have made great strides in identifying the biological and environmental factors that contribute to the development of anxiety disorders. It is now widely accepted that a combination of genetic predisposition and life experiences can increase the risk of developing an anxiety disorder. Studies have shown that certain brain regions, such as the amygdala and prefrontal cortex, are involved in the regulation of fear and anxiety responses.

Furthermore, research has highlighted the role of neurotransmitters, such as serotonin and gammaaminobutyric acid (GABA), in anxiety disorders. Imbalances in these chemicals can lead to heightened anxiety symptoms. This understanding has paved the way for the development of targeted medications that can help regulate neurotransmitter levels and alleviate symptoms.

In terms of treatment, cognitive-behavioral therapy (CBT) has emerged as a highly effective approach for managing anxiety disorders. CBT helps individuals identify and challenge negative thought patterns and develop healthier coping mechanisms. Research has shown that CBT can produce longterm positive outcomes and reduce the risk of relapse.

Additionally, technological advancements have opened up new avenues for research and treatment. Virtual reality exposure therapy (VRET) has shown promise in treating speci c phobias and post-traumatic stress disorder (PTSD). By creating immersive virtual environments, individuals can safely confront their fears and gradually desensitize themselves to anxiety-provoking situations.

Moreover, research is now focusing on the impact of lifestyle factors on anxiety disorders. Studies have suggested that regular exercise, mindfulness practices, and a balanced diet can have a positive effect on anxiety symptoms. These ndings highlight the importance of a holistic approach to managing anxiety disorders, encompassing both psychological and lifestyle interventions.

In conclusion, ongoing research on anxiety disorders continues to expand our understanding of these conditions and provide new avenues for treatment. By uncovering the underlying causes and exploring innovative therapeutic approaches, researchers are offering hope to individuals struggling with anxiety disorders. It is crucial for the general public to stay informed about these advancements, as increased awareness and knowledge can help reduce stigma and encourage individuals to seek appropriate support.

Promising Advancements in Treatment and Understanding

Promising Advancements in Treatment and

Understanding

Inside the Mind: Exploring A - Z of Anxiety Disorders

Inside the Mind: Exploring Anxiety Disorders

In recent years, there have been remarkable advancements in the eld of mental health, particularly in the treatment and understanding of anxiety disorders. These advancements have brought hope to millions of individuals who struggle with various forms of anxiety. In this subchapter, we will explore some of the most promising breakthroughs in the A-Z of anxiety disorders, providing the general public with insights into these exciting developments.

One signi cant advancement in the treatment of anxiety disorders is the emergence of new therapeutic approaches. Traditional methods such as cognitive-behavioral therapy (CBT) and medication have proven effective, but researchers have been actively developing innovative techniques. One such approach is mindfulness-based therapy, which involves cultivating present-moment awareness and acceptance of anxious thoughts and feelings. Numerous studies have shown promising results in reducing anxiety symptoms and improving overall well-being.

Inside the Mind: Exploring Anxiety Disorders

Furthermore, the understanding of the underlying causes of anxiety disorders has also deepened. While it was previously believed that anxiety disorders solely resulted from environmental factors or genetic predispositions, recent research has revealed the role of neurobiology. Scientists have discovered speci c brain regions and neurotransmitters involved in anxiety disorders, leading to the development of targeted medications that can regulate these imbalances.

Moreover, advancements in technology have opened up new possibilities for anxiety treatment and management. Mobile applications and online platforms have been designed to provide individuals with accessible resources, self-help tools, and even virtual therapy sessions. These digital solutions allow people to seek support and treatment from the comfort of their own homes, breaking down barriers such as geographical distance and limited access to mental health professionals.

Another exciting area of progress lies in the concept of personalized medicine. Researchers are now exploring the potential of genetic testing to identify individual variations in drug metabolism, which can help determine the most effective medication and dosage for each person. This personalized approach to treatment minimizes the trial-anderror process, allowing individuals to nd relief faster and with fewer side effects.

Inside the Mind: Exploring A - Z of Anxiety Disorders

In conclusion, the eld of anxiety disorders has witnessed signi cant advancements in both treatment and understanding. From innovative therapeutic approaches to a deeper comprehension of neurobiology and the rise of digital solutions, these developments offer hope for individuals struggling with anxiety. As awareness and knowledge continue to grow, it is essential for the general public to stay informed and engage in conversations surrounding mental health. By doing so, we can collectively support those affected by anxiety disorders and contribute to a more compassionate and inclusive society.

Potential for Early Intervention and Prevention

Anxiety disorders affect millions of people worldwide, causing signi cant distress and impairing their daily lives. However, there is hope in the form of early intervention and prevention strategies that can help individuals manage and even overcome these disorders. By recognizing the signs and taking action early on, we can make a tremendous difference in the lives of those struggling with anxiety.

Early intervention refers to identifying and addressing anxiety disorders in their initial stages. By doing so, we can prevent the disorder from worsening and potentially reduce the impact it has on an individual's life. It is crucial to be aware of the early signs of anxiety disorders, which can include excessive worry, restlessness, irritability, dif culty concentrating, and physical symptoms such as rapid heartbeat or shortness of breath. Recognizing these signs and seeking help early can make a signi cant difference in the long-term outcome for individuals.

Prevention strategies, on the other hand, aim to reduce the risk of developing anxiety disorders altogether. Prevention involves implementing practices and measures that promote mental well-being and resilience. Some key prevention strategies include fostering healthy coping mechanisms, promoting stress management techniques, and creating supportive environments. By equipping individuals with the tools to manage stress and build resilience, we can reduce the likelihood of anxiety disorders developing.

Early intervention and prevention efforts are particularly important when considering the A-Z of anxiety disorders. Each disorder has its unique characteristics and symptoms, but they all share the common thread of causing signi cant distress and impairment. By addressing anxiety disorders early, we can prevent them from progressing into more severe forms and potentially even prevent the development of comorbid disorders.

For the general public, it is crucial to be aware of the potential for early intervention and prevention. Educating oneself about anxiety disorders, their signs and symptoms, and available resources is the rst step. By spreading awareness and reducing the stigma around mental health issues, we can create a society that is more proactive in seeking help and supporting those in need.

In conclusion, early intervention and prevention hold immense potential for individuals struggling with anxiety disorders. By recognizing the signs, seeking help early, and implementing prevention strategies, we can make a signi cant impact on the lives of those affected. By promoting mental well-being, resilience, and creating supportive environments, we can work towards reducing the burden of anxiety disorders and improving the overall mental health of our society.

Chapter 15 Conclusion

Chapter 15: Conclusion

Recap of Key Points

Recap of Key Points

Recap of Key Points:

Throughout this book, "Inside the Mind: Exploring A - Z of Anxiety Disorders," we have delved into the complex world of anxiety disorders, aiming to provide a comprehensive understanding of the various conditions that fall under this umbrella term. As we conclude our exploration, it is essential to recap the key points discussed in each chapter, ensuring that you, the general public, have a clear grasp of the A - Z of anxiety disorders.

The book began by introducing anxiety disorders as a group of mental health conditions characterized by excessive and persistent fear, worry, and apprehension. We discussed the prevalence of anxiety disorders, emphasizing that they affect millions of individuals worldwide, regardless of age, gender, or socioeconomic status.

Next, we explored the different types of anxiety disorders, starting with the most common one: generalized anxiety disorder (GAD). GAD involves chronic worry and anxiety about various aspects of life, often accompanied by physical symptoms such as restlessness and dif culty concentrating.

We then moved on to panic disorder, which is characterized by recurring panic attacks accompanied by intense fear and physical sensations. Phobias, social anxiety disorder, obsessive-compulsive disorder (OCD), post-traumatic stress disorder (PTSD), and separation anxiety disorder were also discussed in detail, shedding light on their unique features and diagnostic criteria.

In subsequent chapters, we examined the potential causes and risk factors contributing to the development of anxiety disorders. We discussed the role of genetics, brain chemistry, and environmental factors, including traumatic experiences, in triggering anxiety disorders. It is important to note that anxiety disorders are not a result of personal weakness or character aws but rather complex interactions between biological, psychological, and environmental factors.

Furthermore, we explored various treatment options available for anxiety disorders, including therapy, medication, and selfhelp strategies. We highlighted the effectiveness of cognitivebehavioral therapy (CBT) in helping individuals manage their anxiety by identifying and modifying negative thought patterns and behaviors.

Lastly, we addressed the importance of seeking professional help and reducing the stigma surrounding mental health. We emphasized the signi cance of providing support and understanding to individuals with anxiety disorders, ensuring they feel validated and encouraged to seek the help they need.

In conclusion, "Inside the Mind: Exploring A - Z of Anxiety Disorders" has aimed to provide the general public with a comprehensive understanding of anxiety disorders. By recapping the key points discussed throughout the book, we hope to have empowered individuals to recognize the signs and symptoms of anxiety disorders, seek appropriate support, and ultimately live a ful lling and anxiety-free life.

Inspiring Hope for those with Anxiety Disorders

Inspiring Hope for those with Anxiety Disorders

Anxiety disorders affect millions of people worldwide, causing signi cant distress and interference in their daily lives. It is crucial for the general public to understand the various types of anxiety disorders, as well as the potential for hope and recovery that exists for those who are struggling. This subchapter aims to shed light on the A-Z of anxiety disorders and inspire hope for individuals dealing with them.

From generalized anxiety disorder (GAD) to panic disorder, social anxiety disorder (SAD), and speci c phobias, anxiety disorders encompass a wide range of conditions. Each disorder presents its unique set of challenges, but it is essential to remember that effective treatments and support are available.

Inside the Mind: Exploring A - Z of Anxiety Disorders

Inside the Mind: Exploring Anxiety Disorders

One of the key messages to convey is that anxiety disorders are highly treatable. By seeking professional help, individuals can access a variety of evidence-based treatments that have proven successful in managing anxiety symptoms. These treatments may include therapy, medication, or a combination of both. The book emphasizes the importance of reaching out to mental health professionals who specialize in anxiety disorders, as they possess the expertise to tailor treatment plans to individual needs.

Furthermore, the book highlights the importance of support networks and the role they play in inspiring hope for those with anxiety disorders. Friends, family, and support groups can provide a sense of belonging and understanding, fostering a safe space for individuals to share their experiences and learn from others who have overcome similar challenges. Sharing success stories of individuals who have conquered their anxiety disorders can provide hope and motivation to those currently struggling.

Additionally, the chapter explores self-help strategies that can empower individuals to take an active role in managing their anxiety disorders. Techniques such as mindfulness, relaxation exercises, and cognitive-behavioral strategies are discussed, providing readers with practical tools they can implement in their daily lives.

Lastly, the subchapter emphasizes the importance of destigmatizing anxiety disorders. By raising awareness and promoting understanding, the general public can contribute to creating a more compassionate and inclusive society. Encouraging open conversations about anxiety disorders can help individuals feel less alone and inspire hope that they can lead ful lling lives despite their condition.

In conclusion, this subchapter aims to inspire hope for those with anxiety disorders by providing information, sharing success stories, and promoting understanding. By shedding light on the A-Z of anxiety disorders, it empowers individuals to seek help, build support networks, and implement self-help strategies. Through education and compassion, we can create a world where anxiety disorders are understood, managed, and overcome.

Final Thoughts and Encouragement for the Journey

As we come to the end of this enlightening journey through the A-Z of Anxiety Disorders, it is important to re ect on the insights and knowledge gained. Anxiety disorders affect millions of people worldwide, and by understanding them, we can work towards destigmatizing and supporting those who suffer from these conditions.

INSIDE THE MIND - EXPLORING ANXIETY DISORDERS

Throughout this book, we have explored the various anxiety disorders, from generalized anxiety disorder to social anxiety disorder, panic disorder, and many more. We have delved into the causes, symptoms, and treatment options available. However, it is crucial to remember that these disorders are not a re ection of weakness or character aws. They are real medical conditions that can affect anyone, regardless of age, gender, or background.

If you or someone you know is dealing with an anxiety disorder, it is important to seek help from a quali ed healthcare professional. They can provide appropriate diagnosis, guidance, and treatment options tailored to your speci c needs. Remember, you are not alone in this journey, and there is hope for a brighter future.

Inside the Mind: Exploring A - Z of Anxiety Disorders

While the road to recovery may not always be easy, it is essential to remain positive and hopeful. Surround yourself with a supportive network of friends, family, or support groups who can encourage you along the way. Remember to be patient with yourself and celebrate even the smallest victories. Recovery takes time, but with dedication and perseverance, it is possible.

Additionally, self-care plays a vital role in managing anxiety disorders. Take time for yourself, engage in activities that bring you joy and relaxation, and prioritize your mental wellbeing. Practice mindfulness and stress reduction techniques such as deep breathing, meditation, or exercise. These strategies can help alleviate symptoms and improve your overall quality of life.

Finally, remember that you are more than your anxiety disorder. Embrace your strengths, passions, and talents. Cultivate a sense of purpose and ful llment in your life that extends beyond your condition. By focusing on your personal growth and positive achievements, you can reclaim control and live a ful lling life despite the challenges you may face.

In conclusion, the A-Z of Anxiety Disorders is a comprehensive guide that aims to provide understanding, support, and empowerment to individuals dealing with anxiety disorders. By raising awareness and reducing the stigma surrounding these conditions, we can create a more compassionate society. Remember, there is always hope, and with the right resources and support, you can overcome the obstacles on your journey to recovery.

INSIDE THE MIND -

Exploring Anxiety

Disorders"

"INSIDE THE MIND - Exploring Anxiety Disorders" is your essential guide to understanding one of the most common yet misunderstood mental health issues. This book delves deeply into the complexities of anxiety disorders, serving as a valuable resource for sufferers, caregivers, and healthcare professionals alike. This comprehensive guide covers a wide range of conditions from Generalized Anxiety Disorder to Social Anxiety and Panic Disorders. Discover their symptoms, causes, and life-altering effects, all presented with real-life case studies and the latest scientific research. But this book doesn't stop at diagnosis; it explores various treatment options including therapy, medication, and lifestyle changes, empowering you to take control of your mental health.

"INSIDE THE MIND - Exploring Anxiety Disorders" is your essential guide to understanding one of the most common yet misunderstood mental health issues. This book delves deeply into the complexities of anxiety disorders, serving as a valuable resource for sufferers, caregivers, and healthcare professionals alike. This comprehensive guide covers a wide range of conditions from Generalized Anxiety Disorder to Social Anxiety and Panic Disorders. Discover their symptoms, causes, and life-altering effects, all presented with real-life case studies and the latest scienti c research. But this book doesn't stop at diagnosis; it explores various treatment options including therapy, medication, and lifestyle changes, empowering you to take control of your mental health.

www.ingramcontent.com/pod-product-compliance
Lightning Source LLC
Chambersburg PA
CBHW050520160726
48003CB00001B/391